M

Gu
Ge
Go

Gum Geckos and
God

A Family's Adventure in Space, Time, and Faith

James S. Spiegel

ZONDERVAN.com/
AUTHORTRACKER
follow your favorite authors

Gum, Geckos, and God
Copyright © 2008 by James S. Spiegel

Requests for information should be addressed to:
Zondervan, *Grand Rapids, Michigan 49530*

Library of Congress Cataloging-in-Publication Data

Spiegel, James S.,
    Gum, geckos, and God : a family's adventure in space, time, and faith /
James S. Spiegel.
      p. cm.
    ISBN 978-0-310-28353-9 (softcover)
    1. Christianity — Miscellanea. 2. Christian children — Religious life.
  I. Title.
  BR121.3.S74   2008
  230 — dc22   2007049186

Published in association with the literary agency of Wolgemuth & Associates, Inc.

Interior design by Beth Shagene

Printed in the United States of America

08 09 10 11 12 13 • 21 20 19 18 17 16 15 14 13 12 11 10 9 8 7 6 5 4 3 2 1

For Amy, Bailey, Samuel, Magdalene, and Andrew

How blessed I am to have you
as fellow characters in the book that is our lives

Contents

Preface

If you can probe the sticky topics of faith and life's meaning with a kid while he probes the sticky recesses of his nasal cavity, then you can discuss theology with anyone. If the truths of God are revealed even in the eyes of a dragonfly or the molting of a gecko, then God's truth is everywhere. And if even a three-year-old child can sense the love of Jesus, then faith is for everyone. These are some of the conclusions I've drawn from my experience so far as a parent.

I once thought that the best place to learn about God is in a classroom or with your nose buried in a book. Those are important contexts for learning, but all of life packs lessons about the divine. Every domain of human experience can serve as the laboratory of faith. It is possible to lose sight of this fact, especially when you have spent a quarter of a century in school and when much of your time out of the classroom has been occupied with books.

Soon after receiving my PhD in philosophy from Michigan State University, I landed a full-time teaching position at a small liberal arts college in Indiana. Prior to hearing of this opening, I had never heard of Taylor University and was pleasantly surprised by the warm but academically serious environment there. I soon learned to appreciate the school's emphasis on the integration of faith and learning. Professors are encouraged to share their personal faith inside and outside of the classroom.

From the beginning of my professional career, my academic life and personal life overlapped. Prior to my marriage, I had students at my house regularly. A few guys even became roommates. When I married Amy in the spring of 1998, I knew my interactions with students would change, but I still wanted to take a holistic approach to my vocation. One of the ways Amy contributed to this was by visiting each of my classes once a semester with baked treats. Amy enjoyed meeting my students, and the students enjoyed the cookies or brownies (and meeting Amy). When our kids arrived on the scene, the fun really started. The students loved interacting with the kids, and the kids loved the attention.

My job and my home have continued to intertwine, but as my children have gotten older, an interesting thing has happened. While it used to be that my family played a role in my academic life, more and more my work in philosophy and theology has informed my role as a father.

As I've always told my students, great ideas should not just inhabit classrooms; they should permeate our lives. But I never expected that they would find their way into my kids' nightly prayers, be shouted from their sandbox, and become a fixture in our family dinner conversations. I also never knew that topics as wide-ranging as bicycles, gum, and baseball all lead to God. But, as my children have shown me, nothing is too mundane to inspire an inquisitive mind. Without realizing it, my kids have tutored me on how to integrate faith and learning in ways I could never have imagined.

This book might create the impression that my kids are obsessed with issues of faith. That's only because I have condensed here so many of our theological conversations. The truth is that they are pretty balanced kids who spend most of their time riding their bikes, playing in the yard, and building Lego fortresses. However, whenever Amy and I see an opening for some theological discussion, we dive right in. Sometimes we land in the deep well of our kids' hearts, gaining insights into their perspectives on life and God. Other times we hit dry land. This is true of everyone, not just kids. I hope that you walk away from this book seeing that you don't have to be an academic to have meaningful conversations about theology.

As one might expect in a project like this, I took the liberty of embellishing dialogue. Our conversations with the kids tend to veer off into random directions so that to transcribe them directly would have made this book a linguistic maze. In at least one instance, I invented an entire dialogue in order to discuss some issues that needed to be addressed. But all of the events described are true, and the conversations are faithful to our kids' personalities and our family dynamic.

Regarding accuracy, my main concern was doctrinal — to be faithful to Scripture, especially where contemporary ideas, both within and outside the church, have strayed from orthodoxy. Most of the "creedal points" — like the existence and nature of God, the virgin birth, and the divinity of Jesus Christ — are discussed, but so are many doctrinally peripheral issues, some of which will highlight the reasonableness of Christianity and some of which are just fun. But all of it, I hope, will encourage readers in the faith.

What Is God Like?

One afternoon I sat in the back yard listening to the Chicago Cubs on the radio and watching my son Bailey dig for unknown treasures in the sandbox. The sky was sunny, the Cubs were leading, and all seemed right with the world. Little did I know that I was about to be thrown a curveball. The curve came not from a Major League pitcher but from somewhere much more challenging — the mouth of my six-year-old: "Dad, what is God like?" With that simple question began an adventure.

I leaned back in my chair, preparing to spout eloquently. "Good question, Bailey," I said. I had taught philosophy for twenty years, published many books and articles on philosophical topics, and addressed challenging philosophical questions from bright undergrads. But as I searched the mental file for an answer, I realized that never before had I faced such a daunting task as answering my son's straightforward query. "Umm ... That's a *really* good question." The fruit of all of my years of studying and teaching philosophy and theology seemed to evaporate. I had no good answer. "What *is* God like?" I repeated slowly, making my son's question my own.

One of the best question-askers in history was Socrates. His inspiration came one day when the oracle at Delphi declared him to be the wisest man in Athens. Socrates didn't buy it. He went out to disprove the oracle by randomly interviewing his fellow Athenians to find someone wiser than himself. He did so by asking simple questions: What is knowledge? What is goodness? What is beauty? To his dismay, Socrates discovered that while everyone he interviewed claimed to know the answers to these questions, none of them really did. He was the only one who recognized his own ignorance. Hence came his famous assertion: "All I know is that I know nothing." It is wiser to know you don't know than to think you know when in fact you don't know. So, it seemed, the oracle was correct after all.

Socrates' questions — and his radical idea that there is one almighty God, making Socrates, in his polytheistic culture, appear to be an atheist many times over — angered the city leaders. He was arrested and charged with corrupting the youth and inventing false gods. He was convicted and sentenced to death. But he went willingly to his execution — poisoning by hemlock — in hopes that his legacy would inspire others to live virtuously and revere God. For Socrates, philosophy was properly about living, and dying, rightly in God's presence.

Now, nearly twenty-five hundred years after Socrates' death, I and other philosophers pick up his baton, which has been passed from generation to generation. One of the principal tools of my trade is the Socratic question. What is knowledge? What is goodness? What is beauty? When I pose such questions in class, I see students shift uncomfortably in their seats and squeeze their eyes shut for a moment as they struggle for a response. They have never considered such things before. The realization that we don't know as much as we thought we did is just as jarring to us as it was to the ancient Athenians.

"Don't you know, Dad?" Bailey asked, laying aside his shovel and looking up at me expectantly. At six he had yet to learn that there were some answers even Dad didn't know.

"Well . . ." I said at last, "God is sort of like . . . a dad."

"A dad?" my son echoed skeptically.

"Yeah," I said. "Only he's invisible and much more powerful."

"Hmm. That's weird." With that comment, Bailey went back to digging as if willing to let the conversation drop.

Perhaps I should have let it go, but I refused to be intimidated by a little kid who barely knew how to read. I poised myself and contrived an explanation. "Well, think about it. We came from God, right?"

"Right."

"And he takes care of us, right?"

"Uh huh."

"And he loves us and teaches us how to live. Aren't those the sorts of things that a good dad does?"

"Yeah. But I can *see* you. Why can't I see God?"

I reached over and turned off the radio. The Cubs would have to win this one on their own. "Does that disappoint you — that God is invisible?"

"Yeah, sort of," he said timidly.

"Just remember this, Bailey. You are invisible too."

"What?"

"Your soul, I mean. The part of you that thinks and has feelings is invisible. And my soul is invisible too, isn't it?"

"I guess . . ." I was sensing some skepticism on his part, but he squinted up at me, willing to at least hear me out.

"Think about it. Do you see my thoughts?"

"No."

"Do you see my feelings?"

This elicited a look that spoke volumes as to what Bailey thought of the absurdity of my question, but he only answered with "Nooo," drawing out the word like he was speaking in slow motion.

"But my thoughts and feelings are real, just like yours are, right?"

"Yeah." Bailey nodded as he began to comprehend my point. Just then a car rumbled down the street, one of the many mufflerless vehicles that plague our neighborhood.

After glaring appropriately at the offending motorist, I resumed. "Bailey, your soul — it's also called a spirit — lives in your body. We can see your body, but your soul is invisible. And just because we can't see your soul, that doesn't mean it's not real, does it?"

"Right."

"It's the same way with God. He is — "

"The Holy *Spirit*!" Bailey interjected.

"Yes, exactly!" Smart kid. "He's invisible, but he is very real, with his own thoughts and feelings. And he controls the whole world, even better than we control our own bodies."

"Whoa." Bailey looked down at his hands as he pondered this. Palms upward, he slowly clenched and unclenched his fingers, studying their movements. After a moment he looked up again. "Can God do anything, Dad?"

"Yes. Well, he can do anything he *wants* to do."

"Can he make himself not invisible?"

"That's something he wouldn't want to do."

"But *could* he do it if he wanted to?"

"Hmm." I leaned forward in my chair, studying his earnest face. "I'd have to say no."

"Why not?"

"Because to do so God would have to make himself not God."

"Oh." He dropped his head as if disappointed.

I had answered his question, but not his concern. "Why do you want God to be visible?"

Bailey looked up at me with plaintive eyes. "So I can hug him when I see him."

This is one of those moments as a parent when your heart breaks with joy. "Bailey, that is wonderful that you want to hug God. And the good news is that you *can*."

"How? You said God is always invisible."

"Yes, but I didn't say that he can't put on a body. In fact, he *has* put on a body, one just like ours."

"Jesus?"

"That's right."

"But Dad ... um ..."

"Yeah, buddy?"

"Uh ... how will I know him when I see him?"

This one made me smile, and Bailey smiled in response. "Oh Bailey, you'll know him when you see him, I guarantee you that. God will make sure that you can't miss him."

"And he'll let me hug him?"

I nodded. Suddenly all my emotions were in my throat and under my eyelids, so I kept quiet.

Bailey stood up and dusted the sand from his pants. "I think I get it now, Dad."

"Get what?" I asked.

"How God is like a dad."

I smiled and pulled my son over for a hug.

Something people notice about Bailey (now eight) is his keen moral-spiritual sensibility. This first became apparent to my wife and me just a few months before Bailey turned three. We had taken him to his first film at the theater, an animated feature titled *Spirit*. In this film there is a lot of gun fighting, and as we drove home afterward, Bailey began to ask questions about guns and how they kill. When we thought we had satiated his curiosity, there was a long silence, then came his stumbling query: "Why ... we ... *need* guns?"

This floored me for several reasons. For one thing, I was amazed that this question came from the mouth of a two-year-old. For another, it struck me how this question, like so many others of significance, takes us right back to the garden of Eden. But mostly, the force of Bailey's question had to do with a realization I had recently come to, through another film, *Life Is Beautiful*, and my reading of Tolkien's Lord of the Rings trilogy.

In Benigni's film, set in Italy during the Second World War, a Jewish father works diligently to shield his son from the genocidal evil unfolding all around them. He succeeds in doing so, through comedic ploys, all the way through their internment in a concentration camp. The night I watched that film, I cried myself to sleep. It obviously hit me hard emotionally, but the reason for this was not clear to me at the time. During this period, I was also reading Tolkien's books, and I occasionally found myself in tears with his descriptions of the Black Riders, who hotly pursue Frodo and his loyal company of friends. As with the film, I wasn't quite sure why I was so moved by the narrative. I rarely cry watching films, and I had never done so reading a book. But now, all of a sudden, I was a flood of tears! Why? The answer came to me that night in the car, driving home from the film, discussing the subject of guns with Bailey. Again I began to cry, but now I knew why. Bailey's simple query showed me plainly something that the Benigni film and Tolkien's books communicated to me only subconsciously: no matter how hard I try, I cannot completely shelter my child from evil in this world.

My son is sure to encounter deep hatred and even cruelty, through no fault of his own. It is also certain that he will himself become entangled in sin to some degree, since the same poison lurks within us all. On top of this — if Tolkien and the apostle Paul are correct — there are unspeakably evil entities, the *real* Black Riders, that already hate Bailey, though he has done nothing to provoke them. And they are intent on enticing him to become an agent of evil as they are.

With this realization I resolved to emphasize my kids' moral-spiritual training above all else. Nothing can compare to the importance of training my kids to be wise — to understand God and his ways and to live accordingly. The more they can learn about God, the more prepared they'll be to face life's temptations and to outrun the Black Riders who hatefully pursue them. I also glimpsed, all at once, that the greatest practical value of my vocation as a Christian philosopher is how it equips me for this daunting task.

During all of my years in graduate school, never once did I consider how my training in philosophy — the study of wisdom — would enable me to be a better parent. Now I think about it every day.

I love being a parent, but some aspects of the job — and it *is* a job — are truly insufferable. Take dressing the kids, for example. Now that is something I really loathe. I'm normally a patient person, whether it's waiting in line or listening to a tiresome person drone on about his job. But nothing tests my patience like putting clothes on a little kid. Man, it gets me uptight just writing about it. I think it's a combination of two factors that make it so hard for me. There's the sheer tedium of the task itself—first this sock, not this way, but that; no, wait, it's upside down. Okay, now, pull—hard enough to get it over that pudgy foot but not so hard that the knee bends and you lose all leverage. All right, good, that one is on correctly. Okay, now the other sock ... And so on. Seemingly endlessly. The same dull tasks, over and over and over and ridiculously over again—like Sisyphus and his boulder.[1] It seems you just manage to reach the top of the hill, getting your child fully clothed and ready to face the day, when the proverbial boulder rolls down the hill and he spills juice down the front and you have to start pushing all over again.

The resistance that you get from the child as he grows impatient with the process is also nearly unbearable. You're trying your best to patiently put clothes on this squirming kid, and he's losing *his* patience because you're not dressing him quickly enough. The next thing you know, he's moaning and crying, and you want to throw his shoe across the room. But somehow you manage to calmly put it on his foot and successfully tie it. Ah, another small but hard-won victory.

Considering my experiences as a parent, the daily reminders that God is my Father are very humbling. To shield my pride, I sometimes tell myself, "At least he doesn't have to put up with as much whining from me every day as I deal with from my kids." Then it occurs to me that God witnesses not only my spoken complaints but also my private grumblings. A passing thought of resentment about some aspect of my life registers in the divine ear like nails on a chalkboard. And my "private" attitudes of pride and condemning judgments of my neighbors might as well be screaming profanity, as far as the all-perceiving Mind is concerned. These realizations can make you feel pretty immature from a moral standpoint.

But then these darker moments are more than made up for by the seizures of grace that come with parenting. To have a child is to experience a genuinely unique kind of love. People tell you this before you have kids, and you believe them — or you affirm what they are saying in an abstract way — but you really don't understand. I have loved others in all sorts of relational contexts — love of my parents, siblings, extended family, friends, and romantic interests. My love for my wife topped them all. We are wedded soul-to-soul, and I can't imagine having a better life partner. Some of these affections have been more or less natural, but none of these loves has been completely selfless. In fact, for the longest time I had no idea that this was even a possibility for me or any other mortal in this world. Then I had a child of my own.

Before becoming a parent, I used to hear people talk of how readily they would die for their kids. And I would think to myself, "Wow, that's heroic. To give your life for your child — what a noble thing. I don't know if I could ever do that for someone, even if it was my own child." These thoughts seem silly to me now. They reflect a mind that knew nothing of the relational universe in which I now dwell. Every normal and healthy-minded parent knows full well that giving your life for your child, if one had to make such a decision, would not be particularly noble, because no decision would be necessary. The response of self-sacrifice for your own child would be automatic, like blinking or breathing.

In this sense, parental love is its own category of love. In fact, sometimes to me the word *love* seems too soft or gentile, lacking a certain sense of primal compulsion. It's more like a force of nature, an energy that grips you and binds you to your child so relentlessly that you feel at times almost like an automaton or a mindless servant. But, of course, it is no mere force either, because the affection is so deep and resilient. Combine those features and you have, well, parental love, a power so strong that it can compel even the most ordinary person to die for his kids ... or even to help them to put on their socks.

What is God like? Perhaps the reason Bailey's question stumped me initially is because, aside from parents, there are very few things in this world to which God can be compared. As our cosmic parent, he nurtures us continually. And as powerful as parental love is, this is a mere reflection of the one who *is* love.

What awe can be prompted by a six-year-old goofing around in a sandbox. But six-year-olds become seven-year-olds. Their questions multiply, as do the wonders they reveal. Then their little siblings get into the action, and before you know it you're tackling life's biggest questions left and right when all you really want to do is just relax and listen to the Cubs game. Little did I realize what theological realms my kids would lead me into. The conversation was just beginning.

Where Did God Come From?

I'll never forget the day I entered eternity at the children's museum.

My family and I live an hour from Indianapolis. We love small town life, but occasionally we head to the big city for a little action, such as the zoo, the park, or their favorite — the Children's Museum of Indianapolis. Of course, it's never just a little action. It's chaos. When the museum is especially crowded, I find the experience to be a cross between Dante's *Inferno* and, well, Dante's *Inferno*. But the kids love it and, after a few days have passed, they've actually convinced me that I enjoyed it.

The kids' favorite part is the hall of mirrors. One moment you're two feet tall, like Yoda in khakis. The next you're stretched like a piece of human taffy with a head that looks like a pencil. I'm not sure what the museum designers intended for children to learn from the exhibit, but they … okay, we … really get a kick out of it. One day, looking at my own reflection, watching the images shift constantly into ever unique shapes, I had the feeling that I was peering into a different dimension, or several dimensions at once. It occurred to me that I was looking at a metaphor for eternity. The boundless, infinite and forever.

That's where God lives — eternity, just behind the carousel and before you get to the playhouse.

As an undergraduate at Belhaven College, my initial aim was to become a physician. So I majored in biology. But along the way my goal changed — at the hands of a philosophy professor, Wynn Kenyon. A brilliant intellect and superb educator, Kenyon is also lovably quirky: a dry-witted practical-jokester with little sense, or concern, for fashion. On at least one occasion, he inadvertently wore a different style shoe on each foot. He personifies the absentminded-professor stereotype. But he is a man of immense virtue and wisdom, and I made sure to spend as much time as possible around the guy in hopes that some of his wisdom might rub off.

One day in Kenyon's class when discussing an argument for God's existence, a student posed that most hackneyed of all theological riddles: can God make a rock so big that he cannot move it? I shook my head impatiently at the student's query, expecting Kenyon to dismiss it as naïve.

To my surprise, he took off his glasses and began to rub his forehead, as is his habit when deep in thought. "This is an important question for all theists, Christians included," he said. "If God can't make a rock he can't move, then there is something he cannot do, namely make that rock. But if he *can* make a rock that he cannot move, then there is still something he cannot do — he can't *move* that rock. So either way, there is something God cannot do. This apparently silly question is actually potentially devastating to the Christian belief that God is all-powerful. So what is the answer, class? This isn't easy."

I shifted in my seat and leaned forward, realizing he was right. This *wasn't* easy. After a few students responded without much success, Kenyon finally agreed to give us his response. "God can move any rock he can make," he began. "True, this implies he can't make something that exceeds his own power to control it. But, as Thomas Aquinas observed long ago, omnipotence is not the power to do anything at all. Rather, it is the power to do *anything that is logically possible*. To insist that an all-powerful being must be capable of creating an object he can't control is like demanding that he must be able to make a round square or make himself go out of existence. Those are nonsensical demands, and our belief in God is not undermined by them so much as they demonstrate confusion on the part of those who make them."

I shook my head in amazement. "This guy really knows how to *think*," I said to myself. I was hooked. Kenyon's patient and systematic approach to this and many other quandaries in philosophy and theology taught me an invaluable lesson: all questions are worth taking seriously. Little did I know at the time how much this insight would benefit me as a parent all these years later.

My wife, Amy, and I often say that when we met, it was like coming home. We both had some rough roads to travel before finding one another, and our companionship is a true gift. Having children together has only strengthened our bond, even if every day brings a set of new challenges. Unfortunately for both of us, some mornings, just getting up is a challenge for me.

I stumbled down the stairs, my eyes still half-closed.

"Jim ..." She used the tone that says, "You're lucky the kids are here." I was certain she wasn't thinking romance. "You have *got* to get a new alarm clock," she said.

"I know, I'll pick one up this week," I mumbled, plopping myself on the couch in the middle of the kids.

She apparently did not find this answer satisfactory and wanted to emphasize the lateness of the hour.

"I mean, look, it's almost 7:30. The kids have been up for half an hour and are restless."

Now, those of you who don't have children might be saying to yourselves, "Chill out, lady. It's 7:30 in the morning." But in Amy's defense, our kids are early risers. Around 6:30 a.m., you can hear them stirring. By 6:45 the calls of "Can we get up now?" begin, and they have started listening to music on their CD player. After months of trying to ignore them in hopes that they would grow out of it, Amy finally decided the best defense is a good offense. She started getting up before them to have some quiet time before the bustle of the day. She had asked me to get up with them at 7:00 in order to feed them breakfast and lead a family devotion. With every good intention, I had agreed, but sometimes the snooze button got the better of me.

Bailey, Sam (five), and Maggie (three) sat in a pile on top of Amy, while Andrew (one) wandered around the living room, alternating between clearing off the bookshelves and eating leftover popcorn off the floor.

I flashed a quick smile at Amy, a nonverbal apology she accepted with a kiss on the cheek. She handed me her tattered Bible, another casualty of Andrew's wanderings. Who really needs the back cover and the concordance anyway? After one more yawn, I roused myself enough to read a few verses from the gospel of John and comment on them. Then we sang a few verses of "He's Got the Whole World in His Hands" and prayed together. Another day was launched.

This is our daily morning routine, and it rarely goes smoothly. The Bible passages, prayers, and songs sometimes seem like mere punctuations in the more fundamental routine of the kids' fidgeting, jostling one another, heaving sighs, and picking their noses.

On this particular morning, when we were done with our usual effort to muscle a devotion out of this chaos, Sam looked up at me and posed a theological whopper. "Dad, who made God?"

"Who made God?" I repeated, looking down at Sam's eager face. Now I was really awake. Bailey and I had discussed this very issue on a few occasions, so I deferred to him. "Do you want to answer that, Bailey?"

"Okay," Bailey replied without hesitation. The speed at which kids can shift from goofiness to profundity is dizzying. "Sam," Bailey said, "nobody *could* make God, because God made all things. So he would have to make himself. But that's silly, because then he'd have to exist before he existed. Right, Dad?"

"Yeah, that's good, Bailey," I said. Sam lay back on a cushy green pillow, nodding with a slightly furrowed brow.

"Does that make sense, Sam?" Amy asked, as she pried a marble out of Andrew's hand.

"I think so. Nobody made God," said Sam.

"Because nobody *could* make God," added Bailey. The room hung with silence for a few moments — a rarity in our home — then Bailey spoke up again, this time squinting with intensity. "Actually, when you think about it ... and go back and back and back and back and back ... it feels weird to the brain."

Amy and I laughed our approval, and Bailey smiled.

Philosophers are sometimes accused of making people's brains feel weird. We ask hard questions, expose assumptions, and identify fallacies in reasoning. This bothers some folks, even when it's done politely. Socrates did it as a pastime, and it got him killed. Some might say that philosophers are not only an irritant to the brain but a pain in the butt. That's probably true, but then that's a pain we all need at times. All of us are occasionally guilty of shoddy thinking, and if we didn't admonish each other about it, we'd be in serious trouble.

Official "practitioners" of philosophy sometimes make people a bit wary, while others are drawn to them. When I was studying for my master's degree at the University of Southern Mississippi, a friend set me up with a girl named Karen. We went out several times, and when she learned I was studying philosophy, our conversations turned to the deep issues in life. I was fine with that, of course, since I loved talking philosophy and theology, as I still do. But soon I recognized that a shift had taken place. Karen wasn't interested in exploring issues as much as she wanted to pummel me with questions aimed at exposing problems with my belief system. She would ask why I believed in God, why I believed in the resurrection of Jesus, why I trusted the Bible, how I dealt with the problem of evil, and so on. And I would give my best shot in answering her questions.

By our third date, a sorority dance, our time was consumed with discussing apologetics, and I felt like I had become something of a philosophical counselor for her. The evening was about as romantic as a tax-law seminar. Even while grooving to Billy Idol's "White Wedding," my mind was flitting through various objections and replies to theistic proofs.

I could see that Karen's combativeness was coming from somewhere, so I responded to her questions as patiently as I could manage. Finally, after several hours of discussion over the backdrop of eighties music, she became exasperated and said, "Jim, tell me, what would it take for you to *stop* believing in God?"

My replies to her other questions had come rather quickly, but this one stumped me. It dawned on me that I could not imagine *any* scenario that would demonstrate to me that there is no God. This frustrated me at first, because like Karen, I had assumed that since my belief in God is based on evidence, it should be possible that events contradicting that evidence could cause me to surrender my belief in God.

But as I stood there watching the gyrating bodies on the dance floor, it occurred to me that her question was wrongheaded. Belief in God is *not* just about evidence, or at least not in the sense that we usually think about evidence, where, say, data from science, history, or some other source are used to justify a position on an issue. Most of us believe in God because of personal experience. Yes, the reality of God is confirmed by everything from design in nature and big-bang cosmology to near-death experiences and the commonsense belief in moral values. But what really compels most of us is our sense of God's presence with us. My personal experience of God has persisted for many years, working itself out in all of life's details — pleasurable and painful, trivial and momentous.

"*Nothing* could make me doubt God's existence," I finally said to her, reaching for a root beer from the snack table. "That is, so long as my personal history was not erased."

"Nothing?" she said, her voice rising with irritation.

"Perhaps an extreme case of amnesia would do the trick." I smiled. "But short of a deep trauma to my psyche, I can't see it happening. My belief in God is so deeply ingrained that to take it away would completely distort my personal identity."

Karen winced and looked away. After a few moments she looked at me again and said, "Your belief in God is like a tumor whose tentacles invade every vital organ."

"I'm sorry you see it that way," I said, "though that's not the analogy I would choose." I took a sip of my root beer.

"What analogy *would* you choose?"

"I'd say that belief in God is more like blood, which nourishes our vital organs rather than causing them to malfunction."

"For all you know, you *are* malfunctioning as a human being," she said, pointing at me and grinning wryly.

"Maybe, but the idea of malfunction assumes the notion of *proper* function, and this brings us back to the idea of design. See, you can't get away from that ..."

And so we would go, round and round, Karen making her objections and me giving my replies.

That was the last date for Karen and me, but this exchange haunted me for many years. I suppose I felt that I had been unfair or stubborn somehow by declaring that my belief in God is unshakeable. Shouldn't a fair-minded believer at least be open to the idea that his faith is misguided? Isn't it possible that theists are wrong in their belief in God? Or was Karen asking too much of me, or any theist for that matter, to offer conditions for abandoning faith?

It wasn't until several years later that I realized my stubbornness did not reflect merely my personal (and potentially pathological) psychology. Sure, all of my experience confirmed the reality of God, but there was something deeper going on here. What I finally discovered was that the fact of the universe itself proves God.

The philosopher Martin Heidegger once asked, "Why is there something rather than nothing?"[2] Like the rock paradox posed by my classmate in college, this question might first appear silly or trifling. But it actually points to something profound. Since something exists, something must *always* have existed. If ever there was just nothing, then there would still be just nothing. As Dr. Kenyon used to tell us, and as I'm sure he still says today, you can't get something from nothing. Or, in Latin — everything sounds cooler in Latin — *ex nihilo, nihil fit* ("out of nothing, nothing comes"). Therefore, since something exists now, it follows that something must *always* have existed; there is an eternal being of some kind. But more than this, I can conclude that it is the *nature* of that something to exist. Since it has always existed, it cannot be explained by anything else, which is why thinking about it made Bailey's brain feel weird. It can only be explained by itself.

The question that remained was this: Just what sort of being are we talking about here? What is it, exactly, that has existed from all eternity? I discovered that in the history of philosophy there have been only two basic answers to this question — which is nice, because I always get confused by too many options. They are *matter* and *mind*. Either the fundamental reality is matter (some sort of physical stuff) or it is a mind (a conscious supernatural spirit). The first option, known as naturalism, won't do because scientists, even the atheistic variety, tell us that the physical universe *came into existence* in what is called the big bang, roughly fourteen billion years ago, most believe. So what we are left with is *an eternal Spirit who created the universe.* And if I'm not mistaken, that's just the kind of being we label God.

My response to Karen's question, then, was not stubborn after all. I simply couldn't give up my belief in God so long as something — anything at all — existed. Of course, this can be a very difficult concept to grasp. It stretches the mind like a reflection in the hall of mirrors. But hey, that's the nature of eternity.

3

Where Does God Live?

It was dark, and all around me I could hear the sounds of wild animals — mainly crickets. On a Friday evening, my boys and I were preparing to spend the night in the fort I built in the back yard — a double-decker, complete with a slide, cleated ramp, trap door with interior ladder, and a shingled A-frame roof.

I like to build stuff. In my line of work, it's nice to have a hobby in which you see the tangible results of your labor and can say, "There, it's finished." That's not possible in education. Sure, you can see students long after they graduate, and they seem to be living decent, productive lives. But you never know for sure how much you had to do with their success, and for all you know, their lives will one day be a mess. So building things like a cool fort helps to alleviate some of my desire to know I've accomplished something.

Ever since last autumn, when I built the fort, I promised the boys we'd spend the night in it. But when summer came, the days were just too long to do it. Sundown didn't come until 9:00 or 9:30 p.m., which is way past their bedtime. And it just didn't feel right settling in for the night when it was light outside. But by late September, nightfall was coming earlier, and we decided to give it a go. I gathered the sleeping bags, some extra blankets, the flashlight, and a portable radio. The Cubs were closing in on a playoff spot, so I wanted to monitor the scores. It took a bit of effort just to situate ourselves on the floor of the second level. There are two openings, one that goes to the slide and the other to the ramp. I didn't want Sam rolling down either of these in the middle of the night, so Bailey and I lay in front of the openings. After a bit of jostling, we finally settled in. Then came Sam's obligatory request. "Dad, can you tell us a story?"

I know my share of good tales, but a child's insatiable appetite for stories can quickly drain your resources. So one learns to make them up on the spot, to spin yarns so wild and protracted that you surprise even yourself with the things you can dream up — tales about animals, monsters, soldiers, aliens, and anything else that comes to mind, whatever it takes to entertain the kids as they drift off to sleep. But this takes a lot of effort, and I wasn't in the mood for a spontaneous narrative.

Fortunately, two days earlier I had had an experience that provided me with some fresh material.

"Did I tell you guys about the possum I saw the other night?"

"What possum?" Sam shot back, already excited.

"The one in the garage," I said, speaking slowly for dramatic effect. I propped myself up on one elbow so I could see the boys better.

"Not really, right?" said Bailey.

"No, I'm serious. I had a close encounter with a possum two days ago."

"Wow, cool," said Sam.

"Where was he?" Bailey asked, with a hint of skepticism still in his voice.

"In the garage. When I came home from my meeting at the church, I pulled in the driveway and could see two brightly shining eyes looking at me from the back of the garage."

"His eyes were shiny?" asked Sam, sitting up in his sleeping bag.

"They looked shiny, because the car's headlights were on him. They reflect light like a bicycle reflector."

"Cool!" Sam exclaimed.

"What was he doing in there?" said Bailey, forgetting to be skeptical.

"He'd been going through the trash. I guess he's the one who has been digging in the trash cans and making a mess. I really need to get some tops for those trash cans."

"So what did you do, Dad?" asked Bailey. He sat up and leaned back on the wall of the fort.

"I parked the car and left the headlights on, then walked over to him to try to shoo him out of the garage. But he ran from me and climbed up that small roll of carpet in the back of the garage. He worked his way inside it but didn't realize that his rear end was sticking out."

"Why did he do that?" asked Sam.

"Mmm. To hide from me, I guess. I suppose he thought I couldn't see him because he couldn't see me."

"That's silly!" Bailey laughed.

"Yeah, it is. But possums are pretty dumb animals."

"So then what happened?" asked Sam.

"I walked over to him and grabbed his tail," I said, making a grabbing motion with one hand for emphasis.

"Ooh!" cried Sam.

"Why?" asked Bailey.

"I just did it for a second to see what it would feel like. Since his head was far down inside the carpet roll, I knew he couldn't bite me, and that might be the only chance I'll ever get to touch a possum."

"What'd it feel like? Was it *gross*?" asked Sam.

"No, it just felt like a big rat tail—kind of rubbery, with a little bit of hair."

"Cool!" said Sam.

"That *is* gross. Did he try to get away?" asked Bailey.

"Sort of. He burrowed further into the carpet roll. So I picked up the whole thing, with the possum inside, and carried it out of the garage. I placed it on the lawn, then unrolled the carpet, and suddenly the possum was just sitting there exposed, looking up at me."

"Then what'd he do?" asked Bailey, his hands tightening on his knees with excitement.

"He just ran off into the bushes near the house."

"Does he live in there, Dad?" asked Sam.

"I think so."

"Cool!" they said in unison.

"Well, cool for him, maybe. But not cool for us, if he keeps scrounging around in our trash."

We sat there quietly for a few moments, listening to the crickets. Then Bailey said, "Dad, are you sure that possum was a boy?"

"Actually, I'm not. Now that I think about it, the possum did look more like a girl when I grabbed its tail and saw its underside."

"Ooh, so she might end up having little babies," Bailey said, and Sam stiffened with excitement. Suddenly a chill ran through me as I considered the prospect of a possum infestation at my house.

"Let's hope not, Bailey."

"Why?"

"One possum is enough for me to deal with. So don't you go introducing that gal to any boy possums, okay?"

Bailey smiled. "Okay, Dad."

It was about eight o'clock but already nearly dark. I made a mental note to myself that September is the perfect time of year to camp out. Neither too hot nor too cold, and nightfall syncs perfectly with the boys' bedtime.

"Dad?" Sam said, scooting over to get a better look at me.

"Yeah, buddy?"

"Is God a boy or a girl?"

"Oh, that's a good question, Sam. He's not really just one or the other."

"Is he both?" asked Bailey.

"Sort of. He made men and women in his image, so there's a sense in which that's true. But he isn't limited to being just male or female. Men and women both reflect God, but not in all of the same ways."

"Dad, where does God live?" Sam asked. I couldn't help but smile, both at his question and with relief that he'd moved on to different theological territory.

"God is everywhere, Sam," I said.

"Then how come I can't see him?" There was frustration in Sam's voice.

"Because he's a spirit."

"Does he have a body?" asked Sam.

"No."

"No skeleton?"

"No."

"No blood?"

"Nope."

"What about Ben Hur?"

"What?" I said.

"He had blood on him," Sam observed intensely. I was confused.

"Jesus, Dad," Bailey interjected. "He's talking about Jesus—you know, in the *movie*." We had watched the classic Charlton Heston film many times together. And I thought all they cared about was the chariot race sequence.

"Oh, yes Sam, of course. Yeah, Jesus does have a body, and he *is* God. But God the *Father* doesn't have a body."

Sam was silent, and I could tell I'd lost him.

Thankfully, Bailey jumped in. "Dad, if God doesn't have a body, then how can he be everywhere?"

"Here's the thing. You don't need a body to be somewhere. Spirits can be places too."

"That's weird. But spirits are invisible, right?"

"Yes, but remember that you're a spirit too," I replied, tapping Bailey on his knee.

"Right."

"Am I a spirit too, Dad?" Sam asked.

"Yes, you too. And me too. We're all spirits."

"But *we're* not invisible," said Bailey.

"That's true, pal. And why are we visible?"

"Cuz we have bodies!" shouted Sam.

"Exactly. Good one, Sam. We have bodies. And do you know why God gave us bodies?"

"Why?" asked Sam.

"So we can see each other and touch each other and stuff," said Bailey.

"That's right," I said.

"And smell each other!" snorted Sam.

Bailey and I laughed.

"I can smell your toot, Bailey. Huh hah!" said Sam, poking Bailey's back with his foot.

"Quit it, Sam. That wasn't me. That was *you*. You smell your own toot."

"Guys — " I said.

"I smell Bailey's toot. It stinks."

"No, you don't. It's Dad!" said Bailey. They both roared.

"You guys, c'mon. Nobody tooted." We all laughed and then fell silent for a few moments. A cool breeze blew through the fort. I climbed inside my sleeping bag, and then the boys did the same. I could see the moon peeking through one of the sycamore trees in our yard.

"Dad?"

"Yes, Sam?"

"Do possums toot?"

"Yeah, I suppose they do. I think all mammals do, and possums are mammals."

"Does it stink?" said Sam.

"Sure," I said. "But let's finish what we were talking about. Why did God give us bodies?"

No answer. It appeared the flatulence tangent had killed our discussion. Then finally Bailey replied, "So we can be together."

"Bingo. We couldn't really relate to each other if we didn't have bodies, could we?"

"Is that why Jesus put on a body?"

"Yes, Bailey, that's an excellent point," I said.

"Then why doesn't God always have a body? Why is it just God the Son — Jesus?"

"Why do you think?" I replied.

"Cuz he's too big," said Sam gleefully.

"Sam, that's silly," said Bailey, suddenly perturbed.

"Actually, buddy, that's not a bad answer," I said.

"What?" Bailey rolled over and looked at me, wrinkling his face with curiosity. "How can that be a good answer? God can't be big or small, because he doesn't have a body."

"Well, that's true. But remember we said that God is everywhere, right?"

"Uh huh."

"And to be everywhere is to be big in a sense, isn't it?"

"I guess."

"What do you think, Sam?"

"Sure." When Sam says it, the word sounds like "show."

"But when you're in a body, you can be in only one place, right?"

"What do you mean?" asked Bailey.

"Well, for example, Mommy is in the house right now. She can't be in the house and out here at the same time, can she?"

"Oh yeah. I see."

"So if God was always just in a body, then he couldn't be everywhere all the time, could he?"

"No."

"So for God to be everywhere, he had to be a pure spirit and not limited to a body."

"That's cool," said Bailey.

"You're dang right it's cool," I said. "But because he wanted to give us a chance to interact with him with our hands and eyes and ears, God the Son put on a body and became Jesus."

Bailey nodded slowly, staring up at the flashlight I had hung from the apex of the fort's ceiling.

"But, you guys, this also meant that Jesus could be hurt just like we get hurt."

"Yeah," said Bailey ponderingly.

"Did Jesus bleed, Dad?" asked Sam.

"Yes, Sam, he did bleed."

"Did he toot?" Sam wasn't smiling. It was a sincere question. But Bailey rolled his eyes.

"Yes, Sam, he tooted … and burped and sneezed and ate and drank and slept and did all the things that we do every day."

"But he was perfect," added Bailey.

"Exactly. He never sinned."

"Is that cool?" Sam asked.

"Yes, that's definitely cool, Sam," Bailey assured him.

We sat there in silence, staring up at the ceiling of the fort. The air had grown chillier, signaling the approach of autumn.

"Dad, tell us another story," Sam said.

"Okay, just one more." I told them about a badger named Jeff who got lost after he accidentally wandered onto a boat on the Mississippi River. He didn't get off the boat until he was several hundred miles from his home in the woods. His journey back was a painful and troubled one, taking him through all sorts of perils — storms, hunters, and ferocious animals. But with the help of some kind animals, he eventually arrived home again to a sweet reunion with his family. This is the basic structure of most of my spontaneous tales, and the kids never grow weary of it. This night they listened intently for a good fifteen minutes before finally conking out.

When I was sure the boys were sleeping soundly, I grabbed my little radio and turned it on to check baseball scores. The Cubs had won. So, for me, this was the perfect night.

How Much
Does God Know?

Children have a special gift — like ESP, but of a very specialized sort. They can sense with extraordinary accuracy the moment when you are least able to hold a conversation, and at that moment they ask a question of great urgency. On one of our Saturday morning runs to Lowe's, Bailey's distraction meter suddenly picked up a strong signal.

I am a cautious driver. My wife would call me uptight. So when I dropped my travel mug in my lap, spilling hot chai on myself while driving down a two-lane highway, I was more than a little distracted. Naturally, Bailey burst forth with an especially urgent question.

"Dad, when can I watch *Revenge of the Sith*?"

"In a few years, buddy." I knew there was no way this answer would settle the question, but a guy's got to try, especially when trying to clean up a spill while negotiating traffic at fifty-five miles per hour.

Bailey and Sam are really into Star Wars. After renting the DVDs numerous times, we finally purchased the whole trilogy — the original three films, that is. Over the past year, they have watched each episode dozens of times. And when they're not watching the films, they're playing with their Star Wars Lego sets or video games. They just can't get enough of it. We've let them watch two of the more recent films in the series as well — episodes 1 and 2 — but Amy and I refuse to let them become as obsessive about those as with the earlier, classic films.

It is not as though the worldview in the latter films is any more theologically sound than in the others. All of the movies feature George Lucas's distinctively modern brand of pantheism, where the Force not only pervades everything but can be manipulated by those properly initiated. The main difference is that the old Star Wars films are morally inspiring in a way that the more recent ones are not. And the old ones are also vastly superior from an artistic standpoint. We believe it is important to nurture aesthetic taste in children from the outset.

"Why not now?" Bailey asked. "I've watched all the other ones."

"It's too violent." Here I was actually taking Amy's word for it, since I had yet to watch episode 3. Because she's watched more movies than Roger Ebert, I felt it was safe to trust her opinion, which was a definite thumbs down.

"But so are the other ones. *Lots* of people get killed in those." I am sure he and Sam could quickly give me an episode-by-episode body count.

"I know that. But your mother and I just think it's too much in that last film."

"Too many people die?" he asked, looking into the rearview mirror for my response.

"Well, no, it's not how many people die."

"So it's how they're killed?" Bailey asked.

"Um, in a way, yes." The feeling of authoritarian il-logic began to rise in me — something every parent is familiar with. After all, you can explain only so much to a seven-year-old. Sure, he can comprehend the meta-physics of the divine nature, but try explaining to him the logic behind parental censorship of home videos. Good luck.

"What do you mean?" Bailey pressed.

Having now avoided a wreck despite the spilled tea debacle, I was feeling unusually confident, so I decided against my usual tactic of telling him to "just trust me." Instead, I'd actually try to explain my reasoning. "That movie shows lots of innocent people getting killed, but it doesn't encourage viewers to think that's a bad thing."

"But I know that's a bad thing," said Bailey.

"I know you know that, son. But it's still not good for you to see it."

"But *you* see it." Who's been tutoring this kid in the rules of logic? Oh wait, that would be me.

"Yes, but I can handle it."

Bailey was quiet for a few moments, and I thought I might have persuaded him. "I can handle it," Bailey finally responded.

"Not like adults can."

"Is there anything bad in the old Star Wars movies?" he asked.

"Yeah, a few things," I said.

"Like what?"

"Well, the main thing we've talked about before. Do you remember what that is?"

"The Force."

"Right, and do you know what is wrong with that?" I said distractedly, turning in front of an oncoming semi. So much for Mr. Cautious Driver.

"It's not really like God?"

"Yes, good. Do you know how it's not like God?"

"I can't remember."

"Think about it. Both Luke Skywalker and Darth Vader can use the Force, can't they?"

"Yeah," Bailey said with admiration in his voice.

"So what does that mean?"

"That it's everywhere?"

"Well, yes, but what else? What does that show us about the Force being good or bad?"

"Um, it's good *and* it's bad."

"Exactly. But is God both good *and* bad?"

"No, he's just good."

"Okay, so there you go. The Star Wars films teach a false view of God. In fact, the Force is not even close to being like God, because it's not a person. Bailey, there is a religion called Hinduism that teaches something like that. It says that God is not really a person."

"That's weird."

"Hinduism also teaches that God is everything, including you and me."[3]

"So they believe bad things are in God too?"

"Actually, they try to get around that by saying evil doesn't really exist."

Looking in the rearview mirror, I could see the puzzlement on Bailey's face. "But everybody knows murder and stealing are bad," he said. "So they must be wrong. Even a kid can figure that out."

"Good point, Bailey!" I declared, stifling my laughter at his last remark. I pulled the car into a parking space at Lowe's. We unbuckled, got out of the car, and Bailey posed one more question.

"Dad, if Star Wars teaches the Force, then why do you let us watch it?"

"There are many other good things in those films that make it worthwhile overall. The older ones, I mean. They are creative, with interesting characters and good lessons about doing the right thing and being courageous."

"But doesn't *Revenge of the Sith* have those good things too?"

"Not nearly as much," I said, grabbing a cart and heading for the paint department.

"How much good stuff does it need to have?"

"I don't know. Look, it's not just that. *Revenge of the Sith* isn't as artistic as the old films."

"How?" he said, jumping on the back of the cart.

"It's hard to explain," I said.

"But why can't you tell me?"

"Bailey," I said, taking a deep breath, "just trust me."

When and how much is it appropriate to play the "trust me" card as a parent? If you don't do it at all and try to explain your reasoning behind every rule, you'll go bonkers, not to mention undermine your authority as a parent. Sometimes kids really do need to take your word for it that they are unable to understand something or that it isn't appropriate for them to know. But if you do it too much, you'll come off as dictatorial and lose out on opportunities to show your children that the rules are not arbitrary but logical. Besides, showing your kids the good sense behind certain rules has a way of strengthening the force of the "trust me" card whenever you do play it.

I've discovered that God often plays the "trust me" card. Sometimes he does it explicitly, as in the wonderful promise in Proverbs 3: "Trust in the LORD with all your heart and lean not on your own understanding;

in all your ways acknowledge him, and he will make your paths straight" (vv. 5 – 6). Elsewhere, the message is more cryptic, as in Deuteronomy 29:29: "The secret things belong to the LORD." But he also explains a lot of things to us, in Scripture, as well as through history and science and in the course of our daily lives. And his good logic naturally makes it easier to trust him.

Our kids often trust us just because we are their parents, and this trust is reinforced as we love and nurture them. God is our cosmic parent, and we must similarly trust him on the basis of who he is, and our trust should grow as he loves and nurtures us through the years. Unlike human parents, God never errs. Yet often it is harder to trust God than other people. This should not be. God deserves our complete trust because he is not only all-loving but all-knowing. Between these two attributes, I think the all-loving nature of God is much easier to grasp, if only because of Christ's act of self-sacrifice on our behalf. But do we have even an inkling of what God's omniscience means?

The other day I was sitting in a faculty meeting, trying not to doze off during some committee reports. As I looked around, I mused over how much each of my colleagues understands about his or her discipline. It occurred to me that if there was a single mind that possessed all of the knowledge in that room, its intelligence would be unsurpassed in human history. I also considered how easy it would be to trust such a person if he or she were to counsel me on some matter. From there I extrapolated: What if that person had all of the combined knowledge of everyone in Indiana? In the United States? Of the entire world population? Even if God had merely the sum of all human understanding, he should be easy to trust. Yet his wisdom and knowledge infinitely exceed the best human comprehension. Still we struggle to trust him. How twisted is that?

Faith is essentially the practice of trust. And our routine failure to properly trust an infinitely wise God reveals something of our own perversity. We all desire to control our circumstances, and faith is a surrendering of that control. So we naturally tend to rebel against faith. But God graciously counteracts this tendency by nurturing us. Like a good parent, he consistently demonstrates his love. And we, like kids, must trust him on this basis.

Dinnertime at the Spiegels is typically a cacophony of clanging pans, running water, sizzling food, and giggling or fussing children. This evening was no exception. As Amy finished cooking the meal, I set the table and plopped Andrew into his high chair and Maggie into her booster seat. After Amy made several loud proclamations that dinner was ready, Bailey and Sam washed their hands and sat down. The whole process sometimes feels like landing a plane through high winds and rain.

"Would anyone like to pray for us?" Amy inquired, catching her breath.

"I will!" Sam volunteered.

"Okay, go ahead," said Amy. We all bowed our heads and Sam began.

"Dear Lord, thank you for this day and for my Spider Man underwear and Star Wars Lego set and all our friends and Gram and Gramps and please help the possum to have lots of little possums so they can have a family and we can play with them in the back yard and don't let the mommy possum get stuck in the carpet so that she dies and can't take care of her babies because that would be so sad. Amen."

"And thank you for this *food*," added Bailey, in a somewhat shaming tone.

"Now Bailey, he's just learning to pray. Be patient, honey," said Amy.

"Yeah, when you were his age, you would go on for the longest time with your prayers," I said as I began to distribute the dinner rolls.

"Really?"

"Oh yeah," Amy affirmed.

"I wanna roll!" demanded Maggie.

"Just a minute, Mag," I said. "That's right, Bailey, especially at bedtime—you'd go for ten minutes sometimes just thanking God for stuff. Here, Maggie."

"Why didn't you stop me?" asked Bailey, suddenly bashful.

"Because that would be rude," said Amy.

"And butt-oo," said Maggie.

"Okay, here's butter for your roll," said Amy, spreading it on as she spoke.

"Besides, Bailey, we can never thank God enough for all that he's given us."

"I want a strawberry," Sam announced.

"May I have a strawberry, *please*," Amy gently corrected him.

"Please may I have one?" Sam asked, pointing at the bowl of fruit.

"Yes, here you go," I said, handing him one.

"Can God read our minds?" asked Bailey.

"Yes, he knows all of our thoughts," replied Amy.

"Then why does he need to hear us thank him when he already knows we're thankful?"

"That's a smart question, Bailey," Amy said. "What do you think?"

"I don't know," said Bailey. "Just because it's a good thing to do, I guess."

"And that's a good answer," I said.

"The Bible says we're supposed to thank God always," said Amy.

"Why?" asked Bailey.

"One reason is because by doing so, we remind ourselves how much God has blessed us. We tend to take our blessings for granted, and thanking God keeps that from happening."

"So we don't get spoiled?"

"Exactly, Bailey," said Amy. By now she and I had dished out everybody's food. Tonight's menu: salmon patties and broccoli with hollandaise sauce — a favorite among all of us, except Maggie, who is our fussiest eater. Or perhaps *selective* is a kinder word, her first choice always being chocolate Ovaltine. She's addicted to the stuff, and Amy and I indulge her habit robotically.

"So, Bailey, prayer is supposed to change us, not to tell God something he doesn't already know," Amy said.

"What does God know?" asked Sam, taking a big bite of salmon.

"Do you mean *how much* does he know?" I asked.

Sam nodded.

"He knows everything, Sam," said Amy.

"Everything?!"

"Yes, everything," Bailey declared. "He even knows how many hairs are on your head and how many spiders are in our basement."

"Cool," said Sam.

"And you know what else?" I said. "God knows how many spiders are in each of the basements in Grant County, and how many hairs are on the heads of all the people in the world, and how many stars are in each galaxy in the universe."

"Dad?" said Bailey, stopping himself to swallow a bite.

"Yeah, pal?"

"Does God know just things right now or does he also know what's going to happen?"

"Good question," I said. "He knows everything that has happened, is happening, and ever will happen."

"But how can — "

"Ah!" Sam yelped, his face contorting with pain.

"What's wrong?" said Amy.

"I bit my tongue," said Sam, his eyes flooding with tears. He hit the table with his fist out of aggravation.

"Now settle down, honey," Amy said.

Then Maggie began to cry in sympathy, as is her habit when either of the older boys is upset.

"It's okay, Maggie," Amy said. "Sam just bit his tongue." Amy patted her as I checked Sam's mouth. His tongue was bleeding slightly.

"Want me to get some ice water for that, Sam?" I asked. "If you put cold water in your mouth, it won't bleed as much."

"No … I mean, sure," he said through the tears. I prepared his ice-water therapy as Amy continued to feed Andrew, comfort Maggie, and monitor Sam's recovery and Bailey's eating. Amy is a remarkable multitasker. She jokes that when the kids are grown, she could start a career as a U.N. peacekeeper and it would probably reduce her stress level.

After dinner, we cleared the table, Amy put Andrew to bed, I made sherbet cones for the rest of us, and we relocated to the front porch. Amy and I rocked in the swing with Maggie while the boys paced around the porch, kicking a miniature soccer ball back and forth.

"So Bailey," Amy said, "what were you going to ask Dad before Sam bit his tongue?"

Bailey stopped kicking the ball and looked up. "I can't remember. What were we talking about?"

"How God knows everything," said Amy.

"Oh yeah. How can God know what hasn't happened yet?"

"Ooh, that's a good one, buddy. What do *you* think?"

"I have no idea," Bailey said, shaking his head and smiling. He gave the swing a hearty push.

"Well, let me ask you something," I said. "Are we going to church tomorrow?" Instinctively I slowed the swing with my feet. We had had enough injuries for one night.

"Is tomorrow church day?" he asked.

"Yes, it's Sunday," I said.

"Then yes," said Bailey.

"But how do you know that? How do you know we'll go to church tomorrow, when it hasn't happened yet?" I said, watching Amy wipe sherbet off Maggie's leg.

"Because we always go to church on Sunday."

"We go to church because first we *plan* to go, and then we *act* on that plan. Right?"

"Uh huh," Bailey said, his attention now fully on me, while Sam played soccer solitaire with the ball.

"Of course, we don't know for sure that we'll go to church tomorrow, because lots of things could happen to prevent us from going, like a flat tire or really bad weather."

"Yeah, or a giant meteor could fall from the sky and squash the church," Bailey added with a twinkle in his eye.

"Right. But if we had perfect control over everything, then we could know now that tomorrow we'll go to church."

"But only God controls everything," said Bailey. He gave his sherbet cone a lick.

"Exactly, which is why he *does* know whether we'll go to church tomorrow," I said. "He knows everything before it happens, because he controls everything."

"Oh, I get it. Like that time we played chess and you said how you were gonna beat me before you even did it."

"Yes, sort of like that. But God doesn't just control things that happen in the world, like they were chess pieces. He made the whole universe, including us, out of nothing. And he keeps everything existing. If he didn't think about the world, everything would disappear." Bailey nodded slowly, struggling to wrap his brain around this thought.

"Is that like gum?" he said at last, making me think I'd completely lost him.

"Like gum?" I asked, as Sam wiggled his way up onto the swing and into Amy's lap.

"Yeah, you know, when you blow a bubble, if you don't keep blowing, it will shrink down to nothing," he explained.

"Yes," I said, impressed.

"That's a good analogy, Bailey," Amy said.

"Or maybe it's like watching a movie on TV," I said. "It shows only as long as the TV is on. If you turn off the TV, the movie stops. The TV is like God, and the universe is like the movie."

"Wow, that's creepy," Bailey said.

"You could say that," said Amy. "Or you could say that God is awesome."

"God is awthum!" Maggie announced, her face covered with orange sherbet.

Awthum indeed.

This whole business of divine knowledge will break your head if you're not careful. Whatever analogies I use with Bailey eventually fail, because God's omniscience actually implies that he transcends time. But how to explain that to a seven-year-old? My brain gets scrambled by the thought, so I'll give him a few more years before I drop that conceptual Rubik's Cube on him. Perhaps at that time I won't even try to explain it so much as point him to biblical passages confirming the idea (such as 1 Cor. 2:7; 2 Tim. 1:9; and Titus 1:2; each of which refers to the beginning of time).

God created time, just as he created space and matter. Someone once said that time is God's way of keeping everything from happening at once. As finite beings, we can comprehend only so much. We must "concentrate" in order to think. But with his infinite mental capacity, God can think about everything all at once. He doesn't need to experience things sequentially as we do. He knows the world in one eternal "moment," comprehending the whole of reality in a single thought. This explains how God can perfectly know the future. All of human history is fully laid out before him, and he directly observes the end of history just as clearly as he does our present moment.[4]

So when God plays the "trust me" card, he does not do so like a bumbling human father limited in understanding. On the contrary, he does so from the vantage point of complete understanding and perfect wisdom. So to trust him is the most sensible thing we can do.

5

Why Do Some People Not Believe in God?

I'm not much for stock car racing, but recently I found myself serving on a makeshift pit crew in my own garage. Bailey loves roaming the block with his friends, riding his bike over to the local grocery store for a Coke, or heading to the library to check out a movie. (I am not sure that my children are even aware of the fact there are *books* available for checkout as well.) So when his bike is out of commission, it is crucial that we get it repaired and back on the road. Recently his chain slipped off its sprocket several times. First he tried to fix it himself, but he quickly became exasperated, not to mention filthy with grease. So I fixed it for him each time, and it was I who got covered with grease. Finally, I adjusted the sprocket — increasing the tension on the chain — so it wouldn't come off again. Now he's back in action and a bit wiser about bicycle mechanics. Whenever I fix something around the house, I try to show the kids what I'm doing so they can become handy or at least gain a better understanding of how things work. In the process they also learn a valuable life lesson: things fall apart.

Because this truth plays out in a variety of ways around our home, Saturday is typically a maintenance day for me. The kids like to play in the fort or the sandbox while I'm doing yard work or fixing things. This is convenient for them, because when they make some sort of discovery, I am ready at hand for them to show it off to or ask me about it.

While mowing the lawn one Saturday, I heard Bailey yell over the roar of the mower, "Dad, check this out!" He was walking briskly toward me with Sam trailing right behind. I shut off the engine.

"Look, Dad — a dragonfly. It's *dead*," Sam declared. Bailey was holding a piece of bark, and perched upon it were the stiff remains of the insect.

I stared at the thing, nodding my appreciation. "Did you know they can hover like helicopters and even fly backward?"

"Whoa," said Bailey, and Sam looked up at me, his mouth agape with wonder.

"And some dragonflies from a long time ago grew to be a lot bigger than that," I added.

"How big?" Bailey asked, his eyes the size of saucers.

"The biggest ones had two-foot wingspans," I said, spreading my hands to show them.

"Cool!" said Sam. "Did they bite? Could they *kill* you?"

"No, I don't think so — not people anyway. I'm sure they killed and ate all sorts of other insects. How would you like to be a beetle or a moth with a huge dragonfly chasing you?" I said, wiping my forehead with my grass-stained shirt.

"No way!" said Sam.

"Its eyes are really big," Bailey said, holding the insect just a few inches from his face.

"Yes," I said. "They have bigger eyes than most insects. But all insects have what are called compound eyes."

"What does that mean?" asked Bailey.

I pointed to the two large half-spheres dominating the head of the dragonfly. "See these?"

"Uh huh."

"Each of those eyes is actually thousands of little lenses. Each of our eyes has only one lens. Insects have lots of lenses in their eyes, each one shaped like a ball that's been cut in half." My sons' interest in all things buggish often gives me a chance to use my background in biology.

"So they can see better?" said Sam.

"Yeah. They can't see as clearly as we can, but they can detect movement really well, which is most important for them. Having all those lenses helps them to see better without being able to move their eyes. You and I can move our eyes, but they can't. So they have all those lenses to make up for that."

"Cool," said Sam, a wide grin spreading across his dirt-speckled face.

"What about the wings? Why are they like this?" Bailey asked.

"See how there are two pairs of wings here?" I said, pointing out the forewings and hindwings. "Dragonflies use them separately, so they can do amazing maneuvers, like hover perfectly still or go in just about any direction. Scientists still don't know exactly how their wings work. But they do know that dragonflies are much better at flying than any machine humans can make."

"Wow, really?" said Bailey.

I reached for the pull cord to start up the mower again. "Yep, they sure are well-designed, aren't they?"

"Oh, yeah," said Bailey, and they both nodded.

"What kind of a mind would dream that up?" I asked rhetorically, returning to my yard work.

Bailey just looked at me, smiling and shaking his head.

Later that day, Bailey and I were sitting together in the back yard on a freshly mowed lawn, watching Maggie and Andrew play in the sandbox as we enjoyed a couple of cold juice boxes and some chips.

"Dad, why do some people not believe in God?" Bailey said, taking a long draw on his drink.

"What do you think?"

"I don't know. It just seems kind of weird. Can't they tell from the world that God made it?" Bailey said, screwing up his face in a dramatic show of bewilderment.

"So do you think maybe the problem is with those who don't believe in God?"

"Maybe," he said hesitantly.

"And what do you think that problem could be?" I prodded.

"Umm ... sin?" he said, scratching at a large mosquito bite on his leg.

"That's exactly right. The Bible says that God has made it clear in creation that he exists and is very wise and powerful. One of the psalms says, 'The heavens declare the glory of God; the skies proclaim the work of his hands.'[5] In another part of the Bible, it says that God's invisible qualities are evident in nature, so no one has an excuse not to believe in him,"[6] I said, hoping I hadn't lost him.

"Does it say why some people don't believe?" There is always another question waiting in the wings.

Before I could answer, Maggie took a handful of sand and dumped it gleefully on top of Andrew's head. After scolding Maggie and comforting Andrew, I returned to our conversation. "What was your question again, Bailey?"

"Does the Bible say why some people don't believe in God?" he repeated.

"Yes, actually it does. The Bible says some people suppress the truth by their wickedness."[7]

"What does *that* mean?" he said with a laugh.

"Well ... it means that just like sand getting in Andrew's eyes would make it hard for him to see correctly, the sin in people's hearts makes it hard for them to see the world and God correctly."

"So they can't think right?"

"Yeah — when it comes to thinking about spiritual things, anyway, their minds are messed up," I said.

"Why?" asked Bailey.

"I think part of it is just the fact that they don't *want* it to be true that God exists." I was keeping an eye on Maggie and the shovel full of sand she was holding dangerously close to Andrew.

"Why not?" Bailey persisted.

"Because they know that if God is real, then one day they'll be judged and punished for the evil things they do."

"So they pretend he's not real?" he asked, continuing to pick at the bite on his leg.

"Maybe it starts out like pretending, but it's more like they're just ignoring him. Then as they push God out of their minds, they convince themselves that he really doesn't exist."

"That's bad. It's like they're lying to themselves."

"That's a good point. And they believe the lie."

Bailey furrowed his brow and shook his head at the idea. I let the idea sit for a moment, not wanting to interrupt his thoughts. A neighborhood girl walked by with her springer spaniel. Bailey and I both waved.

Finally I said, "Remember, Bailey, we have no reason to be proud of the fact that *we do* believe in God, and do you know why?"

"Why?"

"Because it was God who showed himself to us."

"He didn't let us ignore him?"

"Absolutely. He kept us from getting so lost in sin that we'd stop believing in him."

Bailey thought about this for a few moments and then said, "It still seems weird."

"What?"

"That some people don't believe in God."

"Why?"

"Because of crocodiles and birds and the stars and everything else he made."

"It just shows how much sin can damage our minds," I said. Bailey nodded with a sad expression.

Then an analogy occurred to me. "Did you know that your mind is like a bicycle?"

Bailey cocked his head and gave me a goofy stare.

"It's true. Think about it. You remember when the chain came off your sprocket the other day?"

"Yeah," Bailey said, playing with the straw from his now-empty juice box.

"You couldn't ride it after that, could you?"

"No."

"Bikes can't function unless the chain is working properly, can they?"

"No."

"Well, our minds are similar. They were made to function a certain way, and sin messes us up."

"When we sin, our mind-chain falls off?"

"Yeah!" I said. "Or you might say that the more we sin, the more likely it is that our mind-chain will fall off."

"Oh," he said, sounding a little unconvinced.

"Our minds are sensitive. Everything we do and say somehow affects the way we think. Remember that dragonfly you found?"

"Yeah."

"Its wings were designed to function a certain way, weren't they?" I began to gather up the trash from our afternoon snack.

"Yeah, by moving the front wings one way and the back wings another way, it could go in different directions."

"Uh huh, but what would happen if someone cut one of the wings in half?"

"Then the dragonfly couldn't fly very well."

"Yes, and what if all of its wings were cut in half?" Bailey and I started walking toward the garage.

"Then it couldn't fly at all?"

"Correct. And that's like our minds. They were made to function a certain way, and the more we sin, the more they malfunction."

"And then we start believing wrong things?"

"Yes, and then we make even more sinful choices."

"That's scary."

"It is, in a way. This shows how important it is to obey God so that we don't damage our own minds and our ability to think straight."

Bailey and I tossed the potato chip bags and empty juice boxes into the garbage can, then we headed back to the sandbox. Andrew was crying and rubbing his eyes while Maggie stood by looking guilty. Dad and big brother to the rescue.

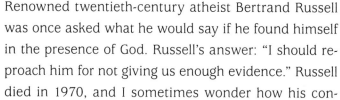

Renowned twentieth-century atheist Bertrand Russell was once asked what he would say if he found himself in the presence of God. Russell's answer: "I should reproach him for not giving us enough evidence." Russell died in 1970, and I sometimes wonder how his conversation with the Almighty went. Who reproached whom?

There are plenty of intelligent people besides Russell who do not believe in God. In fact, in recent years a new strain of atheism has emerged that is particularly aggressive in approach, claiming that religious belief is a delusion, a kind of mental sickness. When I first encountered this claim, I was taken aback. But then it occurred to me that Scripture takes a similar view when it comes to atheism. Those who fail to believe in God are severely deluded, as the biblical language of spiritual blindness suggests.

These are harsh views of the matter, as both perspectives essentially claim that those on the other side are intellectually malfunctioning. But perhaps both sides are correct in casting the issue in such strong terms. To be wrong about the God question is not just to be wrong about some fact or other. It is to be fundamentally mistaken about ultimate reality. And since one's life is steered by what one takes to be ultimately real, to be wrong about God is to have your whole life misguided at a basic level. So it might be appropriate to call such a person delusional, as some contemporary atheists have recently described theists.

But who is deluded, the theist or the atheist? It is worth noting that between the two, the atheists actually make a much more radical claim, if only because the overwhelming majority of people on earth believe in God — more than 90 percent, according to every poll I've seen. So if the new atheists are correct about the "God delusion,"[8] then this is an indictment of the vast majority of human beings. Now, given that belief in

God seems to be so natural, as indicated by these numbers, the new atheists imply that the human mind is not only deeply flawed but naturally so. How else could 90 percent of the human population get it so wrong? And if our minds are so flawed, then they are far from trustworthy. This begs the question, If human beings are naturally prone to form false beliefs about ultimate truth, then why trust anyone's judgment about it? And, of course, this includes the new atheists. So if the new atheists are right about the God delusion, then we have good reason not to trust them!

There is another interesting irony here. From time immemorial, religious folks have been saying that there is something very wrong with human beings, that we need to be fixed at our core and cannot fix ourselves; hence our need for supernatural help. Atheists have long taken offense at this "pessimistic" view of human nature and preach education as sufficient to solve all of our problems. Well, if the new atheists are correct about the nearly universal God delusion, then they have certainly beaten religious people at the game of pessimism. For on their view, there is something deeply wrong with us, but we have no one to fix the problem but our delusional selves.

On the other hand, if God *does* exist and he really *can* cure what ails us, then that is very hopeful. Theists believe that there is an all-powerful, loving God who aims to save us from our plight and grant us eternal bliss with him. The fact that the great majority of people are theists is more hopeful still. On the other hand, atheists believe that this hope is misplaced and that theists are living a lie. Atheists insist that no one can save us and we are all doomed to everlasting personal extinction. So who are the real pessimists here?

Of course, when it comes to belief in God, there is no place for impatience with those who demur. It is not as though one chooses to believe or not believe. One simply finds oneself believing or not. It is something that happens *to* you.[9] So how does one explain the natural tendency to believe in God? John Calvin said it results from the *sensus divinitatis*, an instinctive sense of the divine which normally blooms in full-fledged faith in God as we develop. The *sensus divinitatis* is triggered by many things, from the beauty of nature to our parents' instruction. All of this, you might say, is the result of proper cognitive function. Our minds were designed by God to believe in him, and they will naturally do so unless something interferes with that process, resulting in cognitive malfunction.

Of course, this implies that in the case of the atheist, something has gone wrong cognitively. What could that be? As I emphasized to Bailey, the basic problem is sin. Our spiritual condition affects the way we think. Sin distorts judgment and confuses thought patterns such that truths that should be obvious become unclear or dubious. Sin is especially disruptive when one is thinking about morality or God. Over the years, I have witnessed this truth played out in some grievous ways. I have seen devout believers in Christ succumb to some sin, such as adultery or unforgiveness, and as they refused to repent, their once-orthodox beliefs gradually morphed into deism, agnosticism, or, in some cases, outright atheism. Their wits were beguiled by their sin, confirming Paul's point in Romans 1 — truth is suppressed by wickedness.

Thankfully, the impact of one's moral condition on belief is not just negative. Virtuous living improves us cognitively, as Scripture makes clear. The Lord grants wisdom to the humble and grants understanding to the righteous (see Ps. 19:7; 25:9; Prov. 1:4; 3:32). I have seen this truth demonstrated in some very edifying ways, as men and women who are not especially intellectually gifted mature into profoundly wise and insightful people. Their obedience minimizes the negative impact of sin on their minds. Consequently, they are better able to discern truth and make good judgments.

Socrates famously declared that "to know the good is to do it," as if the causal connection between belief and behavior worked in just one direction. The biblical truth is that it's a two-way causal street. In some sense, to *do* the good is to know it. Our behavior affects our beliefs as much as vice versa. To the extent that we obey or disobey, our ability to think properly will be affected. I find this to be a sobering fact when it comes to the battle against sin. And I pray that God will keep me obedient, lest my mental chain comes off its sprocket!

Fortunately, God sends me daily reminders of his presence, such as my family, friends, sunshine, and even dead dragonflies on a stick.

6

Why Does
God Love Us?

Bailey and Sam came running into the house in a rush of dirt and excitement, startling Amy, who was busy dressing Maggie and Andrew.

"The men cut down a tree in the Shutts' yard — and a mother raccoon and her baby came out!" they exclaimed, one finishing the other's sentence. When the boys have something really interesting to share, they are like two mouths attached to the same brain.

"It looked like there was blood on one of its eyes — " continued Mouth One.

"But probably not," declared Mouth Two. And they both nodded, panting and exchanging glances.

We live in a fairly quiet neighborhood in Fairmount, Indiana, where the felling of a tree can be big news. Amy grabbed Maggie and Andrew, threw them in the stroller, and headed up the street. She had planned to go to the neighborhood grocery anyway, so why not make an adventure out it? The Shutts live next to a church, so Amy and the kids sat on the church steps and watched as the men worked. Two of the Shutts' kids came and sat with them, and soon the boys were rehashing the raccoon story with epic seriousness.

One worker was up a cherry picker, cutting off sections of the towering old maple tree. Unaware of his growing audience, he sawed into another branch. Before long, the enormous limb crashed to the ground, and all the kids gaped.

Amy noticed that the limb appeared solid from the outside, but the inside was virtually hollow, empty except for what looked like dirt. "See that, boys? That tree looked healthy, but inside it was full of bad stuff. That's how some people are. They seem nice but really their hearts are full of sin. People like that are very dangerous."

"What do you mean 'dangerous'?" asked Sam, wide-eyed.

"What would happen if Mr. and Mrs. Shutt just left that tree there?"

"It might fall on their house," replied Sam.

"Or it *could* fall the other way and land on their car," Bailey said after studying the situation.

"That's right. They have to cut the tree down because, though it looks healthy, it's hollow; even a gust of wind could make it fall. If that happened, not only would the tree fall down, but it could hurt someone. It's the same with people. When a person is full of sin, he can hurt a lot of other people as well as himself."

When the men finished cutting down the tree, Amy and the kids headed over to the grocery. On their way back, they saw that the men had cleared out, so Amy stopped to chat with Mrs. Shutt. "I wonder how the tree got so rotten," Amy said.

"Some bugs infested it and began devouring it from within," Mrs. Shutt said. "Then other, larger animals moved in. Once the tree had been weakened by a few small pests, the larger animals could more easily hollow out the tree."

Amy looked at the tree more closely. "Only part of it is rotten," she said. "What a shame to have to cut down the whole thing."

"Yes," Mrs. Shutt said. "It's so pretty and provided shade for the house, which was a relief on hot summer days like today. But the rotten part was near the bottom, and even though everything above it was fine, the rotten part could not support the healthy part. So the whole thing had to be cut down."

As Amy walked home with the kids, everyone a bit sticky from Kool-Aid, she reflected on people she had known who were like that tree, and the damage they left behind. She thought about all those bugs and the raccoons now looking for a new place to live, scoping for a weak spot in another tree. She whispered a prayer for our family and friends — for God's mercy on us and our weak spots — and then went in to make tuna sandwiches.

Early modern scientists used to say that God has written two books, the Bible and nature. Both Scripture and the physical world proceed from God, and each teaches us about him and a multitude of other truths. Christians are accustomed to gleaning counsel from the pages of Scripture, but not enough of us are adept at reading life lessons off natural phenomena. Amy and I believe that nature is embedded with second meanings, life lessons of various kinds. We take our cue from Jesus, who constantly used illustrations from agriculture and the animal kingdom to make his points. The book of Proverbs, too, features instructions based on nature. We are told, for example, "Go to the ant ... consider its ways and be wise! It has no commander, no overseer or ruler, yet it stores its provisions in summer and gathers its food at harvest" (Prov. 6:6 – 8).

One of the most fun things about parenting is discovering these second meanings with your kids, as Amy did with Bailey and Sam in the case of the Shutts' maple. What better image of a wicked person could there be than a tree which has been devoured from the inside? Some people are strong and attractive on the outside but are moral wrecks. They spend a lot of time and energy on their outward appearance or gaining wealth but care nothing about becoming virtuous or wise. They are, as poet T. S. Eliot put it, "hollow men." And when the inevitable storms of life come, they crumble.

Tragically, when the hollow man crumbles, he often takes others with him, including members of his own family. No man is an island, as another poet, John Donne, famously noted. All of our actions reverberate, sometimes affecting entire communities but always affecting those nearest and dearest to us. Like the law of action and reaction in physics, every act, whether good or bad, has some sort of moral impact on the world. Decent and virtuous behavior has redemptive effects, while immoral behavior leads to trouble and broken relationships. Predictably, those who live virtuously are able to see this law of moral reciprocity at work, as they see the connections between their good behavior and the healthy relationships around them. But the wicked are blind to this dynamic and so continue on their destructive ways.

Many proverbs speak to this too, such as the one which says "a man's own folly ruins his life, yet his heart rages against the Lord" (Prov. 19:3). And another vividly contrasts the righteous and the wicked in this regard: "The path of the righteous is like the first gleam of dawn, shining ever brighter till the full light of day. But the way of the wicked is like deep darkness; they do not know what makes them stumble" (Prov. 4:18 – 19).

No one sets out to become a wicked person. I suppose that if we knew Adolf Hitler as a toddler, the last thing that would enter our minds would be the idea that one day he would lead the mass murder of six million people. Yet lurking in the heart of even an adorable child is the same poison which has animated the most brutal people in history. Like trees crawling with insects, we host all sorts of evil thoughts and attitudes — resentment, envy, bitterness, lust, greed, selfishness, and abject pride. These things are universal, but just how much we give in to them is what morally distinguishes people from one another. How much of our core will be devoured by them? And to what extent will these insects of vice give way to the larger beasts of immorality? Hitler's deeds were unique only in their scale. The moral infestation of his soul is the common lot of us all.

I was five or six years old and had just finished swimming at the house of a friend in my neighborhood. As I was heading back to my house, I noticed a small crowd of kids in his back yard. I walked over to discover that they were all gathered around this one kid who was showing off some baseball cards he had just purchased. Having been recently initiated into the world of sports card collecting, I was enthralled. I watched as the boy flipped through the cards, commenting on his favorites while chomping on a huge wad of bubble gum. He also held a dollar which, he made a point of telling us, he planned to use to buy more packs of cards.

Suddenly I found myself overwhelmed with desire, and before I knew it, I had snatched his dollar and was sprinting away, as the kids all yelled at me from behind. Once in my house, I ran into our living room and hid the dollar in a vase. I sat on the couch, my heart pounding and not fully comprehending what I had done. A minute later the telephone rang, and I heard my mother answer. "Hello? . . . Yes . . . Yes, he is. Just a moment." There was a pause, then my mother stepped into the room.

"Jim, did you take some little boy's dollar?"

"Yes," I said.

"Why would you do that? You need to give that *back* right now."

So I fished the dollar out of the vase, and my mom led me out of the house, where I gave it back to the boy and apologized. That day I learned something about the power of envy.

For some reason my boys are fascinated by this story. I'm not sure why. Perhaps they are just amused by the fact that I got into trouble or did something stupid. Or maybe it's because they can identify with the desire to steal. Recently, I probed them a little bit to see if I could figure it out, and at one point I asked them if they had ever wanted to steal something. They both said yes, somewhat ashamed to admit it.

"Did you know that everybody has wanted to steal things?" I asked.

They nodded, as the two of them played with their Legos on their bedroom floor.

"And everybody has had hateful thoughts and has wanted to do mean things. Do you know why?"

"Because of sin?" said Bailey, while carefully fitting a piece onto his X-wing fighter.

"Yes, that's right. We're sinners, and that's why we have those wrong desires. And often people act on those desires, like I did that day when I stole the dollar. But isn't it amazing that God loves us anyway?"

"Why?" said Bailey, looking up at me.

"Why what?" I replied.

"Why does he love us? I mean, we're so bad and everything. I don't see how he *could* love us," said Bailey, his words touched with somberness. He stood up and sat on his bed, opposite me, as I sat on Sam's bed.

"Bailey," I said, pausing to gather my thoughts, "you have to keep in mind a couple of things. For one thing, God doesn't love us because we are good."

"So why does he love us?"

"He loves us because *he* is good. You see, God is love."

"What does that mean?"

"It means that loving others comes natural to him, so much so that he is able to love undeserving people. And did you know there is a word for that — for loving or blessing someone when they don't deserve it? Do you know what that word is?"

"What?"

"Grace."

"Grace?"

"Right. Since we are sinners, we don't deserve *any* blessing. It's all grace, Bailey, every day we live, our health, our family, friends, this house, the food we eat, the music we listen to, all of it."

Bailey stared up at the ceiling, blinking.

"Guys, look at this!" Sam suddenly exclaimed. He was holding up a Lego construction of his own creation.

"What is it, Sam?" Bailey asked.

"It's a battleship, and here's Luke driving it," he said, pointing to a small figure near the front of it.

"Way to go, Sam," I said, and he resumed work on his project.

"So, Bailey, to answer your question," I said, "God loves us because it is his nature to be gracious and to love others. But there's something else that's important to remember."

"What?"

"We are special," I said.

"We are?"

"Yes, you and me. All human beings."

"How are we special?"

"We are made in God's image. Remember how we talked about that? God made us like himself in some important ways. He made us so that we can think and choose and feel emotions, just like he does. Because we are made like him, this makes us precious."

"So he's not wasting his time on something junky, like a broken toy or whatever," said Bailey, giving me a crooked smile.

"Exactly," I said. "I mean, we *are* broken, that's for sure. But we're more like a broken jewel than a broken toy. So I guess you could say that there *is* something in us that deserves God's love. But it's God who put it there, and all those things about us that are precious are only so because they resemble God himself."

"So ... um ... anything that's good is good because it's like God?"

"Yes, that's true. And human beings are especially good because we're more like God than anything else he has made in this world."

"But you said a minute ago that we aren't good. Now you just said we *are* good."

"Yeah, you're right," I said, smiling and realizing the confusion. "Bailey, we are good and not good in two different senses. We are very *good* in the sense that God made us in his image with many wonderful qualities. Even our sin doesn't destroy that. But we are *not* good—in fact we are very bad—in the sense that we are sinners; we make wrong choices and rebel against God. So in terms of our choosing to disobey God, we certainly don't deserve his blessing. Does that make sense?"

"I think so," Bailey said, stroking his chin and looking almost professorial.

"But in the end it comes to the same thing. God loves us because of who he is. Our being made in his image is good because he is so good. And he loves us despite our sin because he is a gracious being."

"So it always comes back to God." As he spoke, Bailey sat up straight and his eyes brightened.

"You said it, big guy," I said, giving his leg a squeeze. And it occurred to me that this was actually a good way of summing up Christian theology. It does always come back to God.

There are Christian writers who avoid discussing sin, insisting that it is more profitable to talk about the love of God. They say sin is too negative and depressing. God's love, on the other hand, is positive and uplifting. What they fail to realize is that divine love cannot be understood without a proper appreciation for the depth of our sin problem. That God loved us "while we were still sinners" (Rom. 5:8) expresses better than anything else just how radical and persistent his love is. And the more corrupted we find human nature to be, the more aston-ishing God's love will prove to be. So rather than being depressing, a realistic doctrine of sin actually plays a critical role in the doctrine of grace, which *is* the most positive and uplifting truth in all of theology.

But let's admit it, the doctrine of sin is not flattering. It is humbling, and none of us enjoy blows to our pride, whether they come in the form of analogies to rotting trees or being lumped in with Adolf Hitler. But once you come to grips with the idea of your own basic perver-sity or screwed-upness — a moral-theological term I just made up — the doctrine of sin itself, even considered independently of divine grace, is edifying in a peculiar way. For me, it has always provided some psychological relief to consider that I'm no worse than anyone else, that my own battles with selfishness, lust, greed, envy, and resentment are typical rather than unique. They say misery loves company, and that's certainly true here: Understanding that you're no worse than anyone else carries with it the hopeful realization that, hey, if anyone can be redeemed, then I can. This might seem like an odd way to look at it, but it has always brought me some hope. Call me a twisted optimist.

7

How Can God Fix Us?

Every parent knows that kids are full of questions and that these questions can be intimidating, especially when the subject is theology. It's as if they're asking, "Dad, I have a question for God. Would you kindly answer for him?" Whoa.

I have found that in following the logical trail of their questions, usually I am led back to the garden of Eden: "Why do people get sick?" "Where did animals come from?" "Why are there bad guys?" And even "Why do we wear clothes?" Proper answers to those questions and many more demand review of the early chapters of Genesis. Revisiting that narrative with my kids' queries in mind has renewed my respect for its subtle profundity, especially when it comes to its implications about human nature. It has also reminded me that most of my kids' questions are not so difficult once you break them down. While they require attention to the Genesis creation story, the proper answers need not be lofty or complex. Well, at least this is true most of the time.

One night while reading to the boys selections from their children's Bible, we covered the story of the fall. When I was finished, Sam said, "Dad, not all snakes can talk, right?"

"That's right, Sam," I said.

"It was just that one snake because Satan was inside him?"

"Yes," I said, as Sam folded his hands behind his head on his pillow.

"But, Dad," said Bailey, "if it was just that one time, then why were all snakes punished for it?"

"Yeah, I would hate to crawl around on my belly all the time!" said Sam, grinning. Bailey smiled too, then continued, "It just seems like only the snake that tempted Eve should be in trouble for it. Anyway, it was Satan who did it. *He* should be punished, not the snake."

"Hmm, interesting. Maybe God was making a point by cursing all snakes in that way," I said hesitantly.

"What point?" said Bailey.

"What is the story really about?" I asked.

"It's about Adam and Eve," he replied.

"Yeah, and what else?"

"The snake!" Sam shouted.

"Yes, that's true too, buddy. But what happened because Adam and Eve sinned?" I prodded.

"Oh, *I* know. The story is about how people became bad," said Bailey, sitting up in his bed. "Adam and Eve disobeyed God and that messed up *everything*." Bailey gestured with his arms for emphasis as he spoke.

"Why did that mess up everything?" asked Sam, his eyes darting between Bailey and me.

"Because we came from them," said Bailey, looking over at Sam. Then he turned to me for confirmation. "Right, Dad?"

"That's right. So now think about the snake."

"Did all other snakes come from that one snake that tempted Eve? Is that why God made them all have no legs?"

"No ... well, actually maybe that's true ... I don't know ... hmm ... good question," I stammered.

"But it doesn't say anything about another snake. There would have to be a girl snake so they could have babies," said Bailey, now looking up at the ceiling.

"A *girl* snake?" blurted Sam.

"Oh wait. Snakes don't have babies. They lay eggs," Bailey corrected himself, slapping himself on the forehead and shaking his head.

"Okay, guys," I said. "The point is that the snake is a symbol."

"A simbo?" said Sam.

"A sym-bol," I said more slowly.

"What's that?" said Sam, knitting his brow.

"A symbol is something that stands for something else. Like this ring here," I said, pointing to my wedding band. "Do you know what it stands for?"

"You and Mommy," said Sam.

"Exactly. It is a symbol for Mommy and me being married. Bible stories contain a lot of symbols. God's curse on all snakes, though just that one tempted Eve, might be a symbol for something. Can you think what that might be?"

"Nope," Sam said, pursing his lips. He and Bailey lay there, waiting eagerly for my answer.

"Bailey, you said it a minute ago," I said. "What is the story about?"

"How people became bad?" he said.

"Right, and what caused that?"

"Adam and Eve."

"Yes, and who did their sin affect?"

"Everybody."

"Yep, everybody — all of us were cursed as a result of their sin. So the part about God's curse on all snakes could be a symbol for that."

"Hmm. That's weird," said Bailey.

"What is?" I said.

"I don't see why *we* should have to suffer when *they* are the ones who did wrong," said Bailey indignantly.

"And you've never done anything wrong?" I nudged.

"Yeah, but *they* started it." Bailey fought back a smile, perhaps noticing the schoolyard logic of his response.

"Yes, but so long as you do wrong, you deserve to be in trouble too. Like when you and Sam mess up your room — it doesn't matter who started it, does it?

"No. But ... why can't we just not sin? Why do we have to sin too, like they did?" said Bailey.

"I think it's because sin is like a disease," I said.

"Like germs?" asked Sam.

"Yes, sort of like that. Only it's not spread like a cold or flu but from parents to their kids."

"When we're born?" asked Sam.

"That's right. It's called original sin."

"What does that mean?" asked Bailey.

"It means that we are all born with a tendency to disobey God. We naturally put ourselves ahead of others and even God. Have you ever noticed that you think of yourself before you think of others?"

"Sort of," Bailey said sheepishly.

"It comes naturally, doesn't it?"

"Uh huh."

"Well, that's original sin."

Bailey's expression had turned very serious. I looked over at Sam to see that he was staring over at Bailey, noting his brother's response.

"Dad," said Sam, finally breaking the silence.

"Yeah, buddy?"

"If we have sin germs, then how does God fix us?"

"Sam, that is a great question. And, really, it's the most important question. But I think you know the answer, don't you?"

He was looking earnestly into my eyes.

"Sam—" Bailey started to volunteer the answer.

"Hold on, let him answer," I said. "How does God fix us, Sam?"

"Um ... Jesus."

"That's right. Jesus came to take away our sin."

"So he's like medicine," Sam said cheerfully.

"Yep, medicine for the soul. Jesus is the cure for sin germs."

Here I had presented only half of the full explanation for original sin, at least as fellows like Jonathan Edwards conceive it. Generally understood, the two aspects of original sin are guilt and pollution. I explained to the kids only the concept of pollution, the natural tendency to sin. The concept of innate guilt is a bit more forbidding and, to modern individualists, downright offensive. The idea is that we are born guilty because when Adam sinned, we all sinned *in* him. This, in turn, is explained by the fact that the human race is unified by our all having descended *from* him. So when God cursed Adam, all of us, his progeny, were cursed as well. His death sentence was our death sentence too. (See Ps. 51:5 and Rom. 5:12 – 17.)

Does that seem unfair? Some people think so. It's easy to be suspicious of the idea when forgetting the doctrine of the second Adam, who is Jesus Christ. But the concept of inherited guilt makes perfect sense when the parallels between the two "Adams" are spelled out. As the first Adam had no human father, neither did Jesus. As we are all descended from Adam, we who are "reborn" in Christ are his spiritual descendents. And as Adam's moral nature (sinfulness) was passed on to us through his sin, Jesus' moral nature (righteousness) is passed on to us through his perfect obedience. (See Rom. 5:18 – 19.) Consequently, Christ's rising to everlasting life is guaranteed to us as well. One could claim that this too is unfair, but I've never heard anyone complain about it.

So through this concept of the second Adam, we understand how the blessings in Christ are applied to us. Funny how a doctrine seemingly so cold and esoteric can turn out to be immensely comforting and practical. And it's another example of how an important truth — in this case a core Christian truth — can be fully understood only by returning to the garden.

When Bailey was four, Amy and I read C. S. Lewis's *The Lion, the Witch, and the Wardrobe* to him. We took turns reading chapters, and Bailey begged for more every night. However, it was hard to tell just how much of it he was catching. As the book's climax approached, I considered how we would explain to him the significance of Aslan's self-sacrifice. How does one broach the subject of atonement with a four-year-old? The fact that the story works as a literary metaphor for this profound theological truth seemed suddenly to make it that much more difficult. I mean, the kid didn't even know the meaning of the term *metaphor*, much less *atonement*.

It fell to me to read the pivotal chapters where Aslan allows the White Witch to slay him and how, through the "deeper magic," Aslan comes alive once more. When I was finished, I put the book down and paused to explain the significance of it all.

"Do you like the story, Bailey?"

"Yeah," he said, nodding and smiling.

"Did you like how even though they killed Aslan, they couldn't keep him dead?"

"Yeah."

"Well, you know, Bailey, it's just like ... You see ... It's like ..." Suddenly, I was at a loss for words. I had no idea how to connect what we had just read with the gospel story. Maybe this is just too much for a four-year old, I admitted to myself. Perhaps we had been wasting our time even reading the book to him.

"It's just like Jesus, Dad," Bailey happily declared.

"Yes!" I exclaimed. "That's right, son, just like Jesus." Somehow, he *got* it, and I was exhilarated — and not just for having been rescued from my faltering attempt at explaining the story's meaning.

Bailey is far from unique in his having understood the gospel at four years of age. In the faith and culture course I teach at Taylor, I often ask students to raise their hands if they became Christians at four years of age or younger. Typically, among the fifty students in the class, at least five hands go up. This is amazing, considering that comprehension of the gospel demands that one understand such weighty moral concepts as duty, sin, punishment, love, and forgiveness.

I am sure there are many parents who are mistaken in thinking that their kids comprehend the gospel. But the point is that many do. And given their stage of cognitive development, this suggests something supernatural is going on. I have known some highly intelligent adults who cannot grasp the concept of grace. They think God's favor is earned by being a good person. That God must forgive them for their sins in order for them to be saved — and that he would do so by redirecting his punishment on his Son — is something they fail to grasp. You might as well try to teach them nuclear physics or differential equations. Why? How is it that a child can grasp spiritual truths that are lost on some otherwise smart adults?

As I mentioned earlier, sin causes cognitive malfunction, and this is especially so when it comes to moral-spiritual matters. The older we grow without being redeemed, the more polluted we are by our sin and the more entrenched we become in our corrupt patterns of thinking. Though by no means pure, children are less corrupted in their thinking and less hardened in faulty thinking patterns simply by virtue of their being younger. So it shouldn't surprise us that the overwhelming majority of Christians come to faith by the time they are eighteen years old.

Another critical factor when it comes to embracing the gospel is explained by Paul when he says, "The man without the Spirit does not accept the things that come from the Spirit of God, for they are foolishness to him, and he cannot understand them, because they are spiritually discerned" (1 Cor. 2:14). Unaided human reason cannot grasp the things of the Spirit. The gospel transcends our natural cognitive abilities. So it appears that the comprehension of the gospel is itself miraculous. Or, you might say, to understand divine grace is itself a work of divine grace.

So there are two major barriers when it comes to grasping and accepting the gospel. One is the spiritual nature of the gospel, which transcends natural reason. The other is our sin, which corrupts cognitive function. The Holy Spirit must graciously overcome both of these obstacles in order to work redemption in any human heart. This implies that all Christian conversions are doubly miraculous and doubly gracious. And given that even after conversion Christians continue to struggle with sin, the Spirit must constantly work to keep us faithful. Job really nailed it when he said that God "performs wonders that cannot be fathomed, miracles that cannot be counted" (Job 5:9).

Bailey was a big fan of the late Steve Irwin, the celebrated Crocodile Hunter. For more than a decade Irwin was a worldwide leader in wildlife conservation, and his irrepressible personality entertained and educated millions of people about animals, especially regarding reptiles. When I received word of Irwin's death, I dreaded telling my son, figuring that he would take it hard. But his response was not what I expected. We were refueling at an Exxon station when I broke the news to him. Bailey asked me how it happened, and I explained that Irwin was stabbed in the heart by a stingray while snorkeling at the Great Barrier Reef off the Australian coast. Watching me pump the gas as he leaned on the hood of the car, Bailey said, "Was Steve Irwin a good man, Dad?"

"Well, Bailey," I replied, "I think he did many good things. He helped a lot of people and animals."

"Do you think he is in heaven now?" he said.

"I don't know. But I do know that if he did make it to heaven, he didn't get there just because of the good things he did. You need to have your sins forgiven to enter heaven, and we can be forgiven only through Christ."

"Did Steve Irwin believe in Jesus?" he said. We both watched the rolling of the gas pump meter.

"I hope so," I said.

"Dad, what if someone believed in Jesus but didn't do good things? Would they go to heaven?"

"You have to have *faith* in Jesus, and that's more than just belief."

"Huh?"

"It's not enough just to believe that Jesus died for you. You need to obey him. Real Christians *love* Jesus, and Jesus says that those who love him obey him. So that's why doing what Jesus says is so important. When we obey him, we prove that we have true faith in him."

Bailey was quiet as I finished pumping the gas, returned the nozzle, and grabbed the receipt. He stood there with his hands in his pockets and a faraway look in his eyes.

"Dad," he finally said, "when I shove Sam or don't share my Legos with him, does that mean I don't love Jesus?"

I squatted down so that I was looking straight at him and said, "Bailey, I know you love Jesus, because you *do* obey him most of the time. And you want to follow him. No one does this perfectly, but you are doing your best, right?" I put my hands on his shoulders, and he smiled self-consciously.

"Remember," I continued, "God is patient with us, and he shows us grace."

The concept of divine grace is risky business. It is essential to the gospel, and to neglect it is to fall into a religion of works. But to give the doctrine proper emphasis can invite abuse. Paul recognized this and posed the rhetorical response, "Shall we go on sinning so that grace may increase?" (Rom. 6:1). He saw how — given our natural sinfulness — we would be tempted to take advantage of grace rather than be inspired by it to live righteously. Of course, his answer is an emphatic "by no means!" To truly live under grace is to be appalled at such a response to God's forgiveness. To presume grace as a license to indulge in sin is a sign that one has not really experienced grace.

To receive God's grace is to be spiritually free, and the essence of this freedom is the ability to obey God. He endows us with his Spirit, by whose help we can live rightly, whereas formerly we were powerless to do so. Thus, our obedience does not achieve our forgiveness but follows upon it. We do not earn our salvation through good works, but our good works prove we are saved. This is Paul's point when he says, "Work out your salvation with fear and trembling" (Phil. 2:12). From the standpoint of human psychology, which of course is fallen, there is a fine line between working *for* one's salvation and working *out* one's salvation. But in terms of biblical teaching, this line must be drawn boldly and decisively.

There is an important sense in which our salvation *is* earned, in which we *are* saved by good works. It's just that we are not saved by *our own* works. Rather, our salvation was earned by the perfect obedience of Jesus Christ. Somehow God applies Christ's righteousness to us, even as he applies our unrighteousness to Christ, punishing him on the cross. So God's grace in Christ consists essentially in an exchange of works. We trade in our evil deeds for Jesus' perfect deeds. Now that's what I call a good deal — and, you might say, good news.

But how, exactly, does this work? Why or how could Christ's merits ever count as our own? And how could punishing Jesus satisfy God's displeasure with us?[10] I think the best answer lies in the concept of mystical union with Christ. As the Holy Spirit unites us with Christ, we are "wedded" to him as his "bride," and we become the "body" of Christ in some strange but real way.[11] Once this mystical union is achieved, we may participate in both his sufferings and his righteousness. By being "in" Christ, we graciously partake in his meriting of salvation.

By the way, this points to another reason why God loves us, one which I neglected to explain to Bailey in our conversation about this. God loves the church because we are *in* Christ. Being mystically united with him, we are made sons and daughters of God. And, of course, any father, including our heavenly Father, loves his children.

But to return to the matter of obedience, how do we go about acting as good children should, we who are infested with sin? Again a crucial part of the answer lies in our union with Christ, which not only justifies us before God but enables us to behave as good children should. Christ's work achieves not only forgiveness of sins but also the transformation of humanity. We who are his children are given a new righteous nature through our mystical union with the God-man. This explains how it is that we can obey God where previously we were powerless to do so. And *that* is how God fixes us.

8

Why Is It Hard to Be Good?

Bailey threw himself onto the living room floor, kicking and screaming and pounding the thick carpet with his fists. Tears poured down his face. He stopped just long enough to point at Amy and shout, "I ... said ... I want ... a brownie!" his words punctuated with spasms of crying hiccups.

"Bailey, I said no," Amy calmly declared. This was followed by more flailing and sobbing.

This was one of the darker scenes from Bailey's life as a three-year-old. Lots of toddlers go through a spell when they throw temper tantrums. Some call it the terrible twos, though it is actually more like two and a half to three and a half. And it's not just terrible; it's hideous. After watching three of my kids go through it, and then suddenly emerge as if from a bad dream, I concluded that there must be a developmental explanation for it. My theory is that during this period, from about thirty to forty months of age, a kid's will far exceeds his or her ability to reason. And their will has one aim: satisfying their own desires. Prior to that time, you can contain the kid without getting much resistance, and after that time, once their rational capacity matures a bit, you can begin to reason with them. But during that span when they are all will and no reason, forget about it. They are Tasmanian devils. No reasoning or disciplining helps. All you can do is wait it out and, of course, *never* give in to their demands. Rewarding a temper tantrum is like feeding a stray cat — a sure way to turn a temporary nuisance into a long-term problem.

When Bailey emerged from his toddler Tasmania, we were surprised to see how morally serious he was for his age. He continued to struggle with his temper, but after his fits he would show genuine sorrow. And he would wonder aloud at how he could get so angry about little things, such as not getting dessert when he hadn't eaten all of his dinner. At one point he asked Amy, "Why is it hard to be good?" Amy gave a response perfectly suited to our three-year-old ethicist. "Bailey, your heart has a good part and a bad part, and whenever you choose to do wrong, you make that bad part a little bit bigger."

"How do I get the bad part out?" Bailey said.

"You can't do it by yourself. You need Jesus to come into your heart and take the bad part away," explained Amy.

That was basically the whole conversation, and we didn't give it much thought until that evening when we were putting him to bed and saying our nightly prayers. Bailey was just learning how to pray, and after going through the ritual "thank you, Lord, for X, Y, Z," he concluded, "and, Lord, please send Jesus into my heart to take the bad part away so I won't do bad things anymore. Amen."

Our hearts burst with joy as we heard this. For what Bailey had done — or what God had done in him — was lay down the gauntlet in his spiritual battle. Refusing to give in to his darker nature, he joined forces with the Light. What Bailey could never know at that age — nor fully comprehend now at eight — is just how costly that alliance is. But neither could he understand — nor do any of us — just how wonderful the eternal payoffs are for those who persevere.

As parents it is our job to fully arm our kids for battle, to train them to be soldiers of virtue. And the paradoxical first lesson is that their first enemy is self. This is a doubly difficult lesson to teach. Not only does it go against our natural tendency to put ourselves first; it defies American culture. Advertisers tell us we can have whatever we want, right now — bigger, faster, better. Politicians declare that we have a right to everything under the sun. Legal firms entice us to sue over anything that bothers us. And psychologists and self-help gurus tell us that focusing on our own needs and desires is the key to mental health and happiness. The result is that we Americans are encouraged to act like toddlers, to be big Tasmanian devils, living always to satisfy our own desires. It's a wonder any of us survive it.

Our boys love animals and are especially fascinated with reptiles. I assume this stems in part from the fact that dinosaurs were reptiles, and — as every parent knows — boys have an innate fascination with dinosaurs. I suspect that for both Bailey and Sam, *Tyrannosaurus rex* was the first polysyllabic term they learned to pronounce.

My wife and I believe it is important for kids to have pets, both from an educational standpoint and for the experience of taking care of another living thing. However, Bailey suffers from severe allergies, so when it came time to choose a family pet, this limited our options to animals of the hairless variety. Our first foray into this arena came when Bailey brought two large bullfrog tadpoles home from school. Somehow I had agreed to this several weeks earlier but had forgotten about it — a common phenomenon around our house; Amy gets irked by how easily I forget things, especially when it involves family plans. What neither of us realized was that it takes bullfrog tadpoles more than a year to mature into frogs. With this revelation, we decided it would be good to give the tadpoles some company. So when

Amy's sister and her family left the country and had to give away their fish, we volunteered to take them.

Suddenly our short-term experiment with tadpoles had turned into a full-blown, long-term investment, complete with aquarium, artificial plants, water filtration system, and two kinds of food — one for the fish and the other for the tadpoles. We had goldfish, mollies, a small catfish, and a miniature freshwater shark. Everything went well for a few weeks, but then the fish, one by one, began to turn belly up. We also had difficulty keeping the water clean, despite trying various products. Fearing that all of our aquatic friends would soon perish, we decided it was in their best interest to set them free. So we deposited them in the private lake of a colleague of mine while he and his wife were away on their summer vacation.

"Why are we here at the Aguilars' house, Dad?" Bailey asked as we climbed out of the car in my colleague's driveway.

"Because we're going to set these guys free in their lake," I said, holding up the large glass jar of fish and tadpoles.

"Did they ask us to do it, Dad?" Sam inquired.

"Not exactly," I replied. We made our way swiftly to the short pier behind the Aguilars' house. Unscrewing the jar top, I added, "Don't you think Mr. and Mrs. Aguilar will appreciate some extra fish and frogs in their pond?"

"Oh yeah," said Sam, rubbing his hands together in anticipation. Bailey nodded.

"And don't you know they'll enjoy listening to the bullfrogs croaking once these tadpoles mature?" I said.

"Yeah ... cool!" Sam exclaimed. Bailey hesitated.

"Dad, my teacher says bullfrogs are really, really loud," said Bailey. "Are you sure the Aguilars — "

"Oh! There they go!" I said, pouring the fish and tadpoles into Lake Aguilar.

"What was that, Bailey?" I asked, grinning deviously.

"Never mind, Dad."

After our fiasco with water pets, we decided that they were not our thing. Why torture fish and amphibians with our incompetence? But then what pet alternatives remained? Bailey's allergies ruled out dogs, cats, hamsters, rabbits, gerbils, guinea pigs, ferrets, and anything else with fur. So what would it be? A turtle? No, too boring. A snake? No, too many negative associations, especially with the whole fall of humanity thing. So it seemed that our pet destiny pointed in just one direction: gecko.

By the time Amy walked out of the pet store with our young leopard gecko, Bailey and Sam had already decided his name would be Toledo. We still have no idea why they chose that name. Kids can be unpredictable, and when you tell them they can name their pet, you have to stick with that commitment no matter how absurd the outcome. Anyway, we figured that Toledo is a cool name, even if it also denotes a dreary industrial midwestern city. Perhaps the name could be redeemed by our little reptilian friend.

Geckos are low-maintenance pets. We outfitted Toledo's terrarium with a stick, rock, water basin, and a piece of hollow wood and he was good to go — a décor both charming and practical. Geckos are very quiet. They make chirping noises when interacting with other geckos, but we've yet to hear any vocalizations.[12] And we probably never will, so long as ours remains a solitary pet. I've also learned that geckos defend themselves against predators by emitting a foul smell and even pooping on them. Now there's a practical skill. But the thing we appreciate most about geckos' excremental habits is the fact that they always defecate in the same place. They select a corner of their enclosure and consistently relieve themselves there. This makes for easy cleanup and also a handy illustration for the kids when potty training: "C'mon, Maggie, if Toledo can always poop in the same place, then so can you, sweetheart."

Geckos eat crickets, meal worms, wax worms, and lots of other small bugs. Whenever I swat a fly around the house, Sam insists that I feed it to the gecko, which I'm happy to do, if only to add some variety to his diet. Feeding a gecko is always entertaining, and the boys love it. You just drop the unfortunate bug into the cage.

The gecko creeps up to it slowly, then lunges lightning fast to capture its prey. A few vigorous chomps and the meal is consumed.

"Ooh, cool!" say the boys. "Give him another one!"

I admit that I find it fascinating as well. There is something about the idea of being eaten alive that is inherently interesting. I've concluded that this traces back to the natural human penchant for tragedy. We appreciate dramas like *Oedipus Rex* and *Macbeth* — not because we enjoy watching others suffer; that would be sadistic. What we appreciate is the realization that that *could* be me while also taking comfort in the fact that it is not me.

Aristotle said tragedies purge negative emotions, like fear and sorrow. Identifying with a character who suffers extreme loss enables one to share in the experience. There is something thrilling about sharing those dark emotions without also having to deal with the consequences of such tragedy. It is satisfying — something akin to relief — knowing one is safe from such loss, if only for now. And of course it is valuable to become more empathetic with those who suffer. Tragedies make us more sensitive to the plight of victims. And they remind us that someday, perhaps soon, we will take our turn. Tragedies are faithful to this deep truth about the human condition, which we are tempted to deny in the business of daily life.

"Aren't you glad you're not that cricket, guys?" I asked my boys while dropping Toledo's next meal into the terrarium.

"Yeah!" they exclaimed, their heads lurching close to the glass to get a better view.

"Just be glad dinosaurs are extinct," I said.

We all stared as Toledo caught sight of the cricket and began to hunt it down. He cornered his prey, then froze midstride, much like a cat would, measuring his final move. Then he darted forward and the cricket was in the lizard's mouth, the insect's rear legs jutting out one side, kicking pathetically. One gulp and the cricket disappeared inside Toledo.

"Whoa, Sam," said Bailey, "just think — that's what a *T. rex* could do to one of us."

"That would be bad," said Sam, nodding intensely at Bailey.

"Are you going to give him another one, Dad?" Bailey asked.

"Yeah, but just one more," I said. "That last one was pretty big." I dropped in another cricket, and the whole scene played out again.

"I'm *so* glad dinosaurs are uh-shink," Sam declared.

"Ex*tinct*," Bailey corrected.

"Yeah," said Sam.

"Guys, it looks like Toledo's starting to molt," I said.

"How can you tell?" Bailey asked.

"See how his colors aren't as bright as normal?" I said, pointing at Toledo. "That's always the first sign."

"Oh, yeah, I see that," Bailey said.

"That's cool," said Sam. "I love it when he molts."

"Maybe tomorrow we'll see him eat his skin," Bailey announced with delight. Sam's eyes widened.

"Could be," I said, "but you'll need to watch him closely, because it's easy to miss."

"How does it work, Dad?" asked Bailey. Toledo began to walk slowly to the opposite side of his enclosure. The three of us studied his movements closely.

"The lizard basically grows new skin from the inside out," I said. "Once a new layer forms underneath, the old skin dries and separates."

"Is that why he looks sort of poofy when he starts to molt?" Bailey said.

"Yeah, and that's why his colors fade so much."

"It's kinda weird," said Sam, cringing.

"Yes, but it's necessary. He has to molt in order to grow."

"Does it hurt?" asked Bailey.

"I'm sure it's irritating," I said. "But it has to be uncomfortable to motivate the lizard to help the process along."

"How does he do that?"

"By rubbing his body against a hard or rough object."[13]

"Like that rock?" said Sam, tapping his index finger on the side of the terrarium.

"Yes, the rock or his log would be good for Toledo to rub against," I said.

"You know what, I think I've seen him do that before," Bailey said. "I wondered why he was doing it. I was afraid he was hurting himself."

"Now you understand the reason for that. So if you see him do it again, you won't be nervous."

"No, I think it'll still bother me, Dad," said Bailey.

"That's okay; I can see why," I said, giving Bailey's shoulder a squeeze. "But just try to think about how it helps him grow and how beautiful he is after he molts."

"That's a good thing to think about, right Dad?" said Sam.

"It sure is." Toledo stepped inside of the hollow log, his favorite place to hang out.

"I also like to think about how he eats his skin. That's so cool," said Sam.

"Yeah, why does he do that?" asked Bailey.

"For nourishment. It's good for him," I explained.

"I think it's gross," Bailey said.

"Have you ever eaten one of your fingernails?" I asked.

"Yeah," said Bailey, hesitantly.

"I ate a piece of my toenail the other day!" said Sam.

"Okay, then you guys are more like Toledo than you think!" I held up the container of crickets. "So maybe we should start feeding you these too," I said.

"Eeeeww!" they both screeched.

Score one for Dad.

Molting is a natural image for Christian sanctification. Spiritual growth is a process of shedding dead moral skin — bad habits, sins that entangle. In the next world we will shed our sinful nature, when God perfects us in our humanity. For now we can only grow more mature, more "colorful" in our Christlikeness. As we all know, it is an arduous process. God uses hard and rough objects to mature us. But it is our job to cooperate by doing the disciplines of the faith — praying, fasting, studying Scripture, and so on. We must also cooperate by not resenting him for the trials he brings our way — for the difficult people he places in our midst and the pains, large and small, we endure throughout our lives. As James says, "Consider it pure joy ... whenever you face trials of many kinds, because you know that the testing of your faith develops perseverance. Perseverance must finish its work so that you may be mature and complete, not lacking anything" (James 1:2 – 4).[14] Trials are the way to maturity — not an easy teaching to accept, but biblical no less. We must molt. It's the only way to grow.[15]

A lot of folks seem content with being "saved," as if getting to heaven were the whole point of the gospel. Naturally, getting to heaven is an enormous benefit of being a child of God, but the point of God's work in us is transformation into the sort of person who will be *fit* for heaven. Like anyone seeking citizenship in another land, we must go through a naturalization — or super-naturalization? — process to be made ready for service in God's kingdom. Sanctification is that process.

Thankfully, God has promised to complete our sanctification once it is begun. As Paul says, "He who began a good work in you will carry it on to completion until the day of Christ Jesus" (Phil. 1:6). Yet we cannot sit idly by, waiting for it to happen. We must work hard at spiritual formation and building moral muscle, not just for our own sake but for others whom we serve. This means putting sin to death through serious repentance. This was Jesus' point when he declared, "If anyone would come after me, he must deny himself and take up his cross and follow me" (Mark 8:34). Paul's emphasis on this point is just as strong when he says, "I have been crucified with Christ and I no longer live, but Christ lives in me" (Gal. 2:20).

When I was in high school, I worked at an animal hospital, where I did everything from clean cages to assist in surgery. It was difficult and sometimes dangerous work, but it was also educational and exciting. Because animals are unpredictable, I never knew what I would encounter each day. Our clinic was primarily a small animal practice, treating dogs, cats, and birds, though we would also get the occasional surprise visit from someone wanting our vet to take a look at a horse or pig. Sometimes our work became exotic, such as when we would vaccinate and do blood tests on wild cockatoos, flown in directly from Australia. You have to pay attention when handling those birds, because they are deceptively strong and can quickly bite off a finger. Once, during a lapse in my concentration, one of them lunged for my hand and, fortunately, came away with a test tube instead, which immediately exploded in its powerful jaws. That was the last time I let my guard down with a cockatoo.

In addition to the pets we treated, our clinic also took in some stray dogs and cats, which we would try to place in homes. When our indoor animal cages filled to capacity with borders, we would place the strays in our outdoor cages. One evening when I was closing up and double-checking the outdoor cages to make sure the clinic dogs had adequate water, I noticed one of the dogs barking frantically and acting strangely. It was staring down at the concrete floor of its cage and stepping about nervously. As I came closer I saw what appeared to be a rope, and just as I reached the cage, the dog mouthed it with agitation and quickly swung it back to the concrete. That is when I realized it was not a rope the dog was tangling with. The snake moved almost imperceptibly, and its mangled body was covered in blood. But even its sluggish movement was enough to give me a chill.

I composed myself and tried to calm the dog, who was still barking hysterically. Needing some way to finish off the snake, I looked around and found something perfect for the job — an L-shaped rebar rod lying only a few feet away. Taking the rebar in hand, I slowly stepped into the cage. With all of the grace and steadiness of a professional diamond cutter, I lowered the heel of the rod onto the base of the snake's head, then applied my full weight to that poor creature's limp body. I felt the crunch of vertebrae beneath me as I twisted my weapon home.

All that remained was for me to concoct some means of displaying my prize for the clinic staff the next day, especially our receptionist, Debbie, whom I and the other kennel cleaners loved to torment with practical jokes. I fetched a ten-gallon aquarium and used the iron rod to put the snake into it. I placed the bloody carnage at the front desk with a note that read, "This is Henry the snake. He's having a bad day and could use a friend."

When I came to work the next afternoon, I was surprised to learn the snake was still alive. I asked Debbie how "little Henry" was doing. She just shook her head and deadpanned, "Very funny, Jimbo." Kathy, our veterinary technician, instructed me to dispose of the snake, now caked with blood. But she sternly cautioned me, for she was certain that what I had captured was the most venomous species in the region, a water moccasin. She told me to dump it into the creek that ran by the clinic, from which it presumably originated. Initially I had planned to pick up the snake using a pair of pliers or hemostats, but I decided to heed Kathy's advice to be cautious.

I carried the aquarium to the riverbank and capsized it above the water's edge. I gave the aquarium an extra shake because the partially hardened blood worked as an adhesive. Though I attempted to drop the snake into the water, instead it plopped onto the mud by my feet. There it sat, seemingly dead. So I kicked it nonchalantly into the gently rolling stream. To my horror, upon hitting the water, the snake wriggled, then suddenly darted off to the opposite side of the creek, swimming with all the vigor of perfect health. A wave of chills wrapped my body as I watched the snake make its way onto a limb that drooped onto the water's surface. I stood and stared at the thing for several minutes, not quite believing what I'd seen.

I ran back into the clinic and found Kathy preparing a leg splint for a cocker spaniel. I explained what I had just witnessed with the snake, but she was unfazed.

"Jimbo, you can't be too careful with a moccasin," she said, focusing on her taping of the splint. "Those suckers are real survivors."

"But Kathy," I said, "I basically crushed the base of its skull last night. I don't see how it could survive that."

Kathy looked at me with an amused grin. "I guess you learned something today. Let me tell you a rhyme that my dad told me when I was a little girl growing up on the farm: a moccasin ain't dead till you chop off its head."

Words to live by.

Although repentance is difficult, we must not underestimate the Holy Spirit's power to help us. Neither should we underestimate the urgency of turning from sin. I think of the Lord's ominous statement to Cain in Genesis: "Sin is crouching at your door; it desires to have you, but you must master it" (Gen. 4:7). Frightening language when you think about it, words which often recall to my mind the cockatoo and water moccasin at the animal hospital. Sin is like that wild bird — you can't let your guard down for a moment. And sin is also like that snake. It ain't dead till you chop off its head.

Do unto What?

"Stop it."

"You stop it."

"No, *you* stop it."

"Stop it!"

"Maggie!"

"Stop it, Sam!"

"Stop—"

"Hey, hey, hey!" Amy said, as she walked into the dining room where Maggie and Sam, both seated at the table, were pointing at each other with their spoons. A Cocoa Krispie hung from Maggie's bottom lip.

"Mom, Maggie was smacking!" Sam bellowed.

"You were smacking, Sam!" Maggie shouted back.

"Okay, you two settle down right now," Amy said, speaking with the intense whisper that indicates she means business. "If either of you yells again, you will get no snack before lunch." Maggie and Sam exchanged scowls.

"She smacked first," Sam said quietly, peering out beneath a furrowed brow.

"Mom—"

"Just a second, Maggie. Let me tell Sam something, then you can speak," said Amy. "Sam, did you smack your food too?"

"Yeah, but she did it first."

"I understand that. But you did it too, didn't you?" Amy put her hand on Sam's shoulder as she spoke.

"Yeah, but—"

"Hold on, Sam. If you don't like it when she smacks as she eats, then you shouldn't do it either, should you?"

"Well . . ."

"Well what? Remember, you should treat others like you want to be treated, right?"

"Yeah, but she did it, and it's annoying!" Sam said, slapping the table with his hand.

"Sam, settle down. Maggie, you know it bothers Sam when you smack your food. Please don't do that, okay?"

"Okay," said Maggie.

"Both of you chew with your mouth closed. It's rude to make smacking noises. Now you guys say you're sorry."

"Sorry, Sam," said Maggie with a suddenly cheery tone.

"I forgive," said Sam. He took a bite of cereal.

"And Sam, what do you say?" asked Amy.

"Errrm shrrzz," he said.

Maggie giggled.

"Sam, swallow your bite first," said Amy, smiling.

"Mmm ... I'm sorry," came his muffled reply.

"I forgive, Sam," said Maggie, still giggling.

"Now you guys have to remember that if you don't like what the other person is doing to you, then you shouldn't do it back. You need to ask politely for them to stop. Okay, Sam?"

"Okay," said Sam.

"Okay, Maggie?" said Amy.

"Umm, okay," Maggie replied, as she put a finger to her lip and pushed the dangling Cocoa Krispie into her mouth.

Someone once asked Jesus, "Teacher, which is the greatest commandment in the Law?" To which Jesus replied, " 'Love the Lord your God with all your heart and with all your soul and with all your mind.' This is the first and greatest commandment. And the second is like it: 'Love your neighbor as yourself.' All the Law and the Prophets hang on these two commandments" (Matt. 22:36 – 40).

It is interesting that the guy asked Jesus for just the single greatest commandment, but Jesus gave him two in response. Perhaps the upshot is that the two are inseparable. Our lives must be lived in human community, so our behavior always regards both God and other human beings.

The second great commandment has come to be known as the Golden Rule, and versions of this principle can be found in every major religion. Confucius, for instance, said, "Do not impose on others what you yourself do not desire."[16] Jesus' version, however, is not merely negative but positive and thus more demanding. He tells us to "do to others as you would have them do to you" (Luke 6:31). What a simple but profound moral guideline — plain enough for a toddler to grasp but a source of wisdom in every interpersonal situation.

It should be noted that the Golden Rule assumes that the person applying it is basically healthy-minded. For example, a suicidal or masochistic individual is not the sort of person you want acting on this principle. But then again, persons with psychopathologies tend to be oblivious to moral concerns anyway. This is one reason why it's not irresponsible of Jesus, or anyone else, to teach the Golden Rule without qualification.

Another prerequisite for proper application of the Golden Rule is a decent moral imagination. One must be capable of imagining what it is like to be other people in various circumstances. If I am considering making a sarcastic remark to a child, it is not enough for me to consider whether I, as an adult, would mind being on the receiving end of that remark. I must try to imagine what it is like to be a child. Or if I am thinking of making a joke about obese people, again I must consider what it would be like to hear that joke as a person with a weight problem.

Imagination is a mental skill, something that one can improve at, and the chief way to do so is through aesthetic experience. Involvement in the arts builds the imagination by enabling a person to better put herself in others' shoes. This is why the arts are crucial to the Christian life. Aesthetic experience makes us more imaginative and thus better at applying the Golden Rule. One might even go so far as to say that anyone who ignores the arts is morally stunted, because imagination is essential to applying the Golden Rule and this principle is at the heart of morality.

Recently, while reflecting on how much we try to instill the Golden Rule in our kids, it occurred to me that we have never actually told our kids the name of the principle. So while cleaning up in the kitchen after dinner one evening, I asked Bailey, "Do you know what the Golden Rule is?"

"Yeah, it's 'Treat others like you want them to treat you.'"

"Good, I knew you knew that; I just didn't know if you knew the name of it."

"I know," said Bailey, and we both laughed at the cadence of our conversation.

"Do you consciously try to live by the Golden Rule?" I asked.

"Yeah, but it's hard to follow because when someone does something to you that you don't like, you want to take revenge."

"Bailey, what would the world be like if everyone followed the Golden Rule?"

"I don't know."

"Would anyone steal?"

"I don't think so."

"Well," I said, "nobody wants anyone taking their stuff, so no one would steal, right?"

"Yeah, that's true."

"Would anyone lie?"

"No."

"Why not?"

"Because nobody wants other people lying to them."

"That's right. So there would be no lies. Would anyone kill?"

"No."

"Right, and why not?

"Because no one wants to be killed."

"So if nobody stole or lied or killed or did anything else wrong, what would that be like?"

"That'd be heaven."

"That's right. So when Jesus tells us to live by the Golden Rule, he's telling us to live now like we're going to live in heaven. Isn't that cool?"

"Yeah, but it's still hard to live like that."

"Yeah it is.

"Dad, how come it seems like it's harder to be good in little ways than to be good in big ways?"

"What do you mean?"

"I mean, I know I won't steal anything or kill anybody, but sometimes when Sam or Maggie is bugging me, it's easy to be mean to them."

"That's interesting, son. I think it's because we know we'd be in huge trouble if we killed someone or stole something. But we don't always get in trouble for saying something mean, so that makes it a bit harder not to do it."

"Dad, sometimes I feel bad because I get mad at Sam and Maggie, but they can be really annoying."

"I know, buddy. But we need to be patient with them, because they're little. But you know, it's probably true for everyone that one of the biggest challenges in life is putting up with annoying things that people do."

"I sure hope I get better at it."

"You will, son. I can guarantee you that you will."

"Good."

"But I also guarantee you that you'll fail a lot too," I added.

"Ooh, bad." Bailey grimaced.

Welcome to life in a fallen world, kid.

Most gems come from metals or stones, but pearls are an exception. They are organic gems, formed naturally within oysters and other mollusks. Pearl formation is the happy consequence of some interesting features of mollusk physiology. An oyster is a bivalve, having a hinged shell protecting its soft interior body. The shell is formed by a thin organ called the mantle, which secretes a substance called nacre. When a grain of sand or some other foreign substance lodges in between the mantle and the shell, the mantle envelops the irritant in nacre. As subsequent layers are secreted, the result is an iridescent crystalline structure — a pearl. This process can take up to eight years.

What makes the Golden Rule an impossibly high standard for fallen mortals is the fact that no matter how badly someone treats you, you should still treat that person as you would want to be treated. No matter how huge the crime, it is wrong to take revenge. Rebuke an offender, yes — any wise person should wish to be rebuked if she has wronged someone; but vengeance is outside of God's plan.

Furthermore, no matter how petty another person's irritation of you, you must not strike back, even if in a similarly small way. Small retaliation is still retaliation, and it violates the Golden Rule. Many times an irritating person is not being immoral. A person may just be annoying, whether it is their sense of humor, style of dress, or the way they talk. We should love such people even if we don't like them. This too fulfills the Golden Rule and is perhaps the most challenging aspect of observing it.

When we refuse to lash out at those who sin against us, we reflect Christ. When we refuse to criticize irritating people and instead put up with them in a quietly virtuous way, without harboring resentment or ill-feelings, we build character. And over time, we may become so patient and long-suffering as to shine like moral gems. So let us all patiently endure the irritants in our lives. Who knows what pearls of virtue will form in us as a result?

What Was Jesus Like?

One evening, on our way home from a Mother's Day dinner, Amy and I had an interesting conversation with the boys, launched by a simple question from Bailey: "Dad, does God speak English?"

"God speaks all languages, buddy," I said.

Bailey frowned, disappointed at that response.

"Jesus spoke a language called Aramaic," Amy added.

"What color was Jesus' skin?" Bailey asked.

Amy and I began to describe Jesus' likely appearance when suddenly a Middle Eastern man appeared, as if on cue, in the median on McGalliard Street. We began frantically pointing and yelling, "Jesus looked like *that* man! Look out the window, guys! Look! Look! *Look!*" The boys saw him and this time both of them frowned, disappointed. Amy and I exchanged quizzical expressions and the boys were silent ... until the next question, this one from Sam.

"How long was Jesus' hair? Was it like Nathan Bergman's?" Nathan is a cool, teenage drummer at our church and our boys' hero, perhaps the closest thing to the Son of God they can imagine.

"Jesus' hair was probably longer than that," Amy said, again disappointing the boys.

"What color were Jesus' eyes?" Sam asked.

"Probably brown," Amy said.

"Yeah!" Sam, whose eyes are brown, rejoiced, looking over at his brother and smiling, while Bailey rolled his blue-green eyes and looked away.

Only then did the point of their questions become clear to Amy and me. They were probing for something they had in common with Jesus.

The boys pose all sorts of questions about Jesus — where and how long he lived, what he spent his time doing, whether he liked living down here, and whether he was fun to be around. Regarding the last question, I have told them that it depends on what people consider fun. To those who were humble and loved God, Jesus was very fun. But for those who were vicious and hated God, he was not very fun to be around. The same is true today, which explains why people sometimes hate even the most faithful Christians.

When people ask whether someone is fun, they often are inquiring whether the person has a good sense of humor. This connection is apparent in the fact that we use the word *funny* to describe such a person. Laughing is fun; thus we call those who make us laugh fun*ny*. So did Jesus have a good sense of humor? He did not spend his time doing stand-up comedy or telling knock-knock jokes. At any rate, the New Testament doesn't give any such indication, though perhaps the Jesus Seminar will propose this theory at their next meeting. But Jesus certainly did have a strong sense of humor, as revealed in several of his discourses.

To see his humor, however, we must first clarify what makes something funny. One brand of humor capitalizes on a sudden sense of superiority over someone else, typically the "butt" of a joke or prank. So when someone's pants fall down or they get a pie in the face, that's "superiority" humor. Another major category of humor relies on incongruity — a particularly odd juxtaposition of two things, such as a talking animal or a man wearing a dress.

Jesus used both of these forms of humor. During his most famous sermon, the one "on the Mount," he asked rhetorically, "How can you say to your brother, 'Let me take the speck out of your eye,' when all the time there is a plank in your own eye?" (Matt. 7:4). What a ridiculous image, both the visual of a beam of wood sticking out of someone's eye *and* the accompanying picture of that same person probing for a speck in their neighbor's eye. The whole thing is wildly incongruous, and it gives us a sense of superiority over the hypothetical target of Jesus' remark. The only thing that keeps us from laughing is the fact that, well, all of us have been that person. But you have to admit that image is pretty funny.

In another instance, Jesus is addressing the dangers of wealth, and he says, "It is easier for a camel to go through the eye of a needle than for a rich man to enter the kingdom of God" (Mark 10:25). Elsewhere, while addressing the Pharisees' legalism, Jesus declares, "You strain out a gnat but swallow a camel" (Matt. 23:24). Both of these camel gags achieve their humor by combining elements of both superiority and incongruity. Naturally, the appearance of a camel adds to the comic effect. It's a goofy looking animal, and picturing someone trying to swallow one whole should put a smile on anybody's face.

Recently I had an experience with my son Sam which brought to mind yet another bit of Jesus' humor. Sam and I were playing together in a shallow part of the Little River in Townsend, Tennessee, when he lost track of a plastic shovel he was using to dig in the riverbank. I caught sight of the shovel slightly downstream, where it had drifted and become caught in some of the foliage. When I pointed this out to him, he quickly waded over to it and retrieved it. But while he did so, it occurred to me that he was moving into an area where the likelihood of his encountering a snake was much greater than in the more open area. So after he grabbed his shovel, I told him to get away from there quickly, which he did. Afterward, as I briefly imagined the horror of seeing my son bitten by a snake, the words of Jesus came to mind: "Which of you fathers, if your son asks for a fish, will give him a snake instead?" (Luke 11:11). I laughed aloud as this ridiculous incongruity hit me like it never has before — and, likewise, I was struck anew by our heavenly Father's care for us, as is one of the points of this passage.

Normally we don't laugh at such comments from Jesus because the subject matter is so serious,[17] though we might sometimes laugh derisively at the Pharisees or others who are shown up by Jesus. His teachings deal with the most important issues of life, like moral corruption, redemption, divine judgment, self-sacrifice, heaven and hell. These things are not laughing matters. But this doesn't negate the fact that Jesus' words reveal a deep sense of humor.

So to return to the original question, what was Jesus like? Specifically, was he any fun to be around? We may note that the term *fun* also means "enjoyable or pleasurable." Was Jesus the sort of person that one might enjoy or take pleasure in being around? Absolutely, so long as you take pleasure in creativity and good critical thinking; so long as you like to be fascinated or even dumbfounded; so long as you enjoy a really, really good challenge; and so long as you take pleasure in being given hope, the greatest possible hope, in spite of whatever else the world seems to be telling you. If any of these things are true of you, then, sure, Jesus was, and is, fun.

"Dad, what was Jesus like?" Bailey asked me, as we stood in the back yard, taking turns pushing Andrew in his kiddie swing.

"He was like us in every way — that's what the Bible tells us," I replied.

"But Jesus didn't sin like us, right?"

"Yes, that's very important."

"How could he never sin? That seems impossible."

"It's hard to imagine, isn't it?" I stopped Andrew's swing to buckle him in more securely.

"Yeah."

"Well, the reason Jesus could live perfectly is he didn't have a sinful nature."

"What does that mean?"

"It means he wasn't born with a tendency to disobey God. You and I are naturally selfish, but Jesus was not. He naturally obeyed God and did his will."

"So it was easy for him to be good?"

"No, but only because sinful people made it hard for him. They treated him very badly his whole life long and then in the end you know what happened."

"They killed him."

"Yep, and all because he obeyed God perfectly."

"So Jesus wasn't selfish." As Bailey spoke, he resumed Andrew's swinging with a strong push.

"No, not at all. And do you know why? Do you know how Jesus could be human but not be selfish like every other human being since Adam and Eve?"

"How?"

"Jesus' father was not human. Do you know who his father was?"

"God?"

"Right. His mother was human — her name was Mary. But his father was God, which means he wasn't cursed like the rest of us who do have a human father. Do you remember how all the snakes were cursed because of what that one snake did in deceiving Eve?"

"Yeah."

"And how God did something like that with people when Adam and Eve sinned, cursing all of us who came from them?"

"Uh huh."

"Well, the way God decided to curse us was through Adam. He made sure that everyone who had a human father would have the same selfishness that Adam had. That's why it's so important that Jesus didn't have a human father. Otherwise he would be a sinner just like us."

"And, Dad, also he wouldn't be God, right?"

"Yes, exactly. Jesus is divine because his father is divine."

"What's *divine*?" Bailey asked, picking a leaf from a nearby lilac bush.

"To be divine is to be God. You know how you are human because your mom and I are human?"

"Yeah."

"Well, anyone with a human mom and dad can only be human. Jesus had a human mother — "

"But his dad was divine."

"Yes, Jesus is God because his dad is God. That's why he was never selfish, and that's how he could never sin."

This exchange shows the importance of the virgin birth for the doctrine of Christ, sometimes called Christology. If Jesus' father was human, then he was just another human being, complete with a sinful nature like the rest of us. However good he might have been, he would be no more worthy to die for your sins than I would. But of course Christians don't just confess that Jesus was born of a virgin. That's only the crucial negative fact — that his father was not human. There is also the positive fact about who impregnated Mary. The divine lineage of Jesus guarantees and explains his holiness and, thus, why he was worthy to die for us. Peter says that through his work, we have been blessed to "participate in the divine nature" (2 Peter 1:4). Only because Jesus himself is both human and divine is it possible for us, mere humans, to be mystically united with Christ. Nevertheless, even some Christians find it difficult to affirm the virgin birth, and for some seekers it is a decisive obstacle.[18]

Just as the virgin birth is crucial for Christology, so is the dual nature of Christ: Jesus was both God *and* man. Now, when you think about it, this is a bizarre claim. For don't Jesus' divine qualities rule out his being truly human and vice versa? The virgin birth is certainly one of those qualities that might seem to preclude his being human. After all, hasn't every other human being had a human father? Well, no. The first humans, Adam and Eve, had no human father, but they were nonetheless human. To insist that having a human father is necessary for one to be truly human would make it impossible for there to be a first human being. So lacking a human father must not disqualify Jesus from being genuinely human.

Actually, this objection can be met with an observation which applies to all complaints of this nature: not all *common* qualities are *essential* qualities. Just because a quality is typical for members of a certain class of objects does not imply that it is necessary for membership. Take belly buttons, for instance. Nearly every human being has one. But we would still recognize a person's full humanity if he or she lacked this particular scar — and, lest we forget, it is a scar, though it is one we have grown so accustomed to that we hardly recognize it as such.[19] Or suppose a human being is successfully cloned. Would this mean that person is somehow less than fully human? Of course not. Again, just because one's circumstances of conception are unique does not imply that he or she is inhuman. Certainly being a clone, or lacking a navel for that matter, is an interesting novelty, but it's hardly a reason for concluding a person is not human. Similarly, Jesus' virgin birth and divine qualities, radically unusual though they are, do not disqualify him from being truly human.[20]

Scripture clearly teaches that Jesus Christ is divine. John declares that he is co-eternal with the Father (John 1:1 – 2). Paul states that "in Christ all the fullness of the Deity lives in bodily form" (Col. 2:9). And the writer of Hebrews asserts that "the Son is the radiance of God's glory and the exact representation of his being" (Heb. 1:3).[21] The Bible also teaches that Jesus is truly human, as he is depicted as growing, eating, sleeping, talking, weeping, walking, being kissed, and engaging in various other activities typical of human beings. The dual nature of Christ is difficult to understand, and even a child may perceive some logical tension in the doctrine. Both Bailey and Sam have been most impressed with the concept of Christ's divinity, which is no surprise. But once they embraced this idea, the reality of Jesus' human nature became lost on them for a while. Of course, this is sometimes true of many adults as well.

Reading the gospel accounts of Jesus' conversations and physical struggles are good reminders of his full humanity, just as his miracles and resurrection are powerful testimonies to his divinity. When I read these stories to the boys, their questions typically focus on one aspect of his person or the other.

One night Sam captured both aspects in a brief bedtime conversation. "Dad, did Jesus chew gum?"

"I don't think they had gum in Jesus' day," I replied. "But if they did, then I suppose Jesus chewed gum from time to time."

"I think he would like gum. And I also bet he could blow the hugest bubble ever!" Sam concluded cheerily.

Now *that* is orthodox Christology.

As we all know, theological heresies are dangerous. But orthodoxy is dangerous as well, though in a different way. Heresy assaults faith and healthy living. Orthodoxy, on the other hand, is a healthy threat to intellectual pride. The mysteries of the gospel challenge our contentment with human-made philosophies and are hazards in the path of pure reason.

Paul once declared that "the mystery of godliness is great" — an understatement, to be sure. The mystery of Christ himself is perhaps even greater, as my sons were about to show me.

11

How Will We Know Jesus When We See Him?

Is that the cross Jesus died on?" Maggie asked, tugging at Amy's shirtsleeve and pointing up at the large wooden cross hanging on the north wall of our church sanctuary. The worship service was about to start, and Amy and I were corralling our brood into our family's usual spot in the second row.

"No, Maggie, Jesus died on a different cross. But it was a lot like that one," Amy replied.

"Oh," Maggie said, satisfied with her mother's response.

Once we were seated, Maggie moved on to other things, such as doodling and coloring in the bulletin. As for Amy and me, we couldn't get this exchange out of our heads.

On our way home from church, Amy and I reflected together on this question of Maggie's. We observed that, for all its apparent silliness, her query revealed how real

Jesus must seem to her. As we discussed this, Maggie conked out, but Bailey listened intently. Then he posed a question of his own.

"Dad, how will I know Jesus when I see him?" He glanced over at Sam, who, like Maggie, was now asleep.

"I don't think you'll have any trouble picking out Jesus when your time comes," I said.

"Why not? I mean, haven't there been lots of people that look like him? How will I be able to tell him apart from all those other guys?"

"Bailey, that's a good question," said Amy, "but I think God will make it clear to us which one Jesus is."

"How? Will he be wearing a sign or shirt with his name on it? Just kidding."

"Ha!" I grinned at him in the rearview mirror, and he grinned back. "You might not be too far from the truth, Bailey."

"What do you mean?"

"God likes to use signs and symbols for different things, so maybe he'll do that with Jesus. Can you think of some signs God used in the Bible?"

"No."

"Aw, c'mon!"

"I can't. It's too hard," he said, shaking his head.

"Give it a try. What about the sign he gave Noah?" I hinted.

"What sign?"

"His sign that he would not let the world flood again."

"Oh, the *rain*bow," Bailey said.

"Yeah, good," I said. "See, that wasn't so hard."

"Bailey," Amy said, "can you think of some things we do in church that are symbols for Jesus?"

"Like what?"

"What do we eat and drink?" Amy asked.

"Bread and juice . . . communion?" said Bailey.

"Very good. That's another symbol of Jesus," I said. "Of course, it's also more than that, but it does function as a symbol. So maybe God does use some signs and symbols in heaven to make Jesus more clear to people."

"What kinds of signs?" asked Bailey.

"I don't know for sure, but I can think of one sign that he will probably use in one way or another, because the Bible refers to it."

"What?"

"Light."

"Light?"

"Yes. Can you think of why light is a good sign for Jesus?"

"I don't know."

"What do you think of when you think of light, Bailey?" asked Amy.

"Umm . . . I think of good — good things."

"That's right. Light is a symbol for holiness, being perfect. What else?"

"Light means being safe from bad guys who do mean things at night when no one can see. I mean, that's when they steal bikes and stuff."

"Very good!" Amy said.

"Yeah, Bailey," I said. "Scripture says that wicked people are children of darkness. The dark represents evil, while light stands for goodness and purity. And if you are in the light, then you don't have to fear darkness. So that's probably one reason why the Bible also says that 'God is light; in him there is no darkness at all'[22] and why Jesus himself says, 'I am the light of the world.'[23] One time when Jesus was up in a mountain with some disciples, God made him shine like the sun. It just blew away those disciples. They fell to the ground, they were so scared."[24]

"Really?"

"Yep. So to get back to your question, I think one way we'll know Jesus when we see him is because he'll shine so brightly."[25]

"So will he still be human?" asked Bailey.

"Yes, absolutely," I said. "Jesus is now and forever God and man."

"I mean, will he still have a body even though he shines like a light?"

"Definitely," I said. "He'll always have a body, but it will be a very special one."

"Good," said Bailey. "That makes me feel better."

It is important to remember that Jesus did not shed his human body upon returning to heaven. Scripture is clear about this. The book of Revelation, for all its cryptic content, makes this plain with John's extended encounters with the glorified Christ. And even the nature of Jesus' ascension drives the point home. As Luke records it, "He was taken up before their very eyes, and a cloud hid him from their sight" (Acts 1:9). Following this is what I consider one of the more comical scenes in the Bible. As the apostles stood there "looking intently up into the sky," two "men," presumably angels, appeared and asked them, "Why do you stand here looking into the sky? This same Jesus ... will come back in the same way you have seen him go into heaven" (Acts 1:10 – 11). That image of all those guys gazing skyward, dumbfounded, probably with mouths agape, cracks me up every time.[26] At any rate, that Jesus returned to heaven in his body is significant. His having a body is not a bad thing or even a neutral thing. It is a good thing.

The Gnostics saw things otherwise. Gnosticism was an ancient religious movement which saw human beings as essentially divine spirits trapped in material bodies. The Gnostics took a dim view of physical reality, and today, as always, Christians are tempted by this heresy. For some reason, many folks just don't want to believe God when he declared of this world, in all its materiality, "It is good."[27] Yes, this is a fallen world, but it suffers no more of a curse than our souls do. The whole of this earthly domain is fallen, and that includes both our spirituality and physicality. But because of the Gnostic tendency to see the physical as inherently corrupt rather than fallen but redeemable, many of us are inclined to think of Christian redemption in solely spiritual terms. But that is a truncation of the gospel. The work of Christ is *totally* redemptive. Jesus renews both spiritually and physically.

By the way, this teaching has profound implications for how we should approach culture. If Christian redemption extends to the physical realm, then our faith perspective should impact all of our physical activities, from business and science to sports and art. There is no realm of human activity into which the redemptive touch of Christ cannot reach. Our lives should reflect this conviction as we strive to do everything we do, whether at work or leisure, in a distinctively Christian way. This is the relentlessly hopeful challenge of the gospel.

Now back to the matter of recognizing Jesus in heaven. Several months later I brought it up again to Bailey, as he and Sam were looking through their Lego catalogue — at the pages featuring Star Wars figures, of course.

"Bailey, how do you think we'll recognize Jesus when we get to heaven?"

"Easy," he said. "When we look at him, God will just zoom the thought into our minds, 'That's Jesus.' Ooh, Sam, look!" Bailey broke off, pointing at one of the pictures in the catalogue. "There's Jabba's sail barge!"

"Yes! I can't *wait* until we get that one!" announced Sam, pumping his fist.

"But we've got to put our money together, cuz it's expensive," said Bailey.

"Yeah," said Sam, as he took a bite of a peanut granola bar.

"Sam," I said, "how do *you* think we'll be able to recognize Jesus in heaven?" He held up one finger to indicate he needed a few seconds to swallow. I was struck by how adultlike this gesture appeared. Finally, with some exaggerated effort, he swallowed his bite and gave me his answer.

"God can do everything, right?" he said.

"Yeah."

"So he'll just make us know who Jesus is, that's all," Sam said, smiling.

"Hey, that's good, Sam," I said, patting him on the back.

"I just heard it from him," he replied, taking another bite of his granola bar and pointing at Bailey with his thumb. Bailey smiled with satisfaction, as they both resumed scanning the catalogue.

Bailey's thinking on this issue certainly had changed. Where previously he was perplexed, he was now dogmatically confident. Was his faith maturing? Or was this just his way to shut me up fast so he could look at his Lego catalogue? Ah, the mysteries of developmental psychology.

Bailey, Sam, and I like to go on bike rides, usually to Playacres Park here in Fairmount. One Saturday afternoon, while Maggie and Andrew napped, the boys asked if we could ride to the park to check out some recently installed playground equipment. Although the sky threatened rain, I decided we'd go for it. The boys' eagerness to check out the new equipment was irrepressible. Besides, this would give Amy a much-deserved break from the kids.

The park is only half a mile from our house, but the trip there usually takes a good twenty minutes, with all the stops we make along the way to pet — or avoid — dogs, examine bugs, chat with neighbors, or pick up "cool" sticks or rocks. This time our journey went faster than usual, as we began to hear the rumble of thunder not long after our departure. We practically raced to the park, the boys exploding off their bikes on arrival. Together they played on the new play set and some of the other new equipment, but in the end they came back to their old standby — the giant spiral slide. Then the rain came, slowly for the first few minutes, then finally a torrential downpour. Just before the bottom fell out, we ducked under a small shelter near one of the baseball diamonds.

"Whoa, that was close!" said Sam, shouting over the rain.

"Yeah, I'd hate to be out in that," Bailey said, shaking his head. The rain was so heavy that it cast a gray hue as far as you could see. A small river formed in the parking lot, emptying into a drain just a few feet from our shelter. Once the boys noticed it, they moved to the corner of our shelter closest to the drain to get a better look. We stood there watching the rain and listening to the echo of the drain's hidden waterfall.

"Dad," Sam said, still looking down at the drain, "God can stop the rain if he wants to, can't he?"

"That's right, buddy. He sure can."

"Do you think he will?"

"Yes, I do. I just don't know when."

"Yeah," Sam said, looking up at me with a slight grin and rubbing his nose.

"Would it be magic if he made it stop all of a sudden?" Sam asked.

"Well . . . hmm." I paused to collect my thoughts.

"Would it, Dad?" Bailey prodded, intrigued by Sam's question.

"Give me a second, pal. Umm . . . You know, guys, I think I'd say, yes, it would be magic. But you know what else?"

"What?" said Bailey.

"I think it'd be magic even if God didn't stop the rain suddenly. In fact, I think what we're seeing right now, this rain, is magic."

"Why?" Bailey asked, as he patted a puddle with the bottom of his sandal.

"Because God's controlling it. He brought this rain, and everything that God does is magical. But I know what you mean. When God does something really out of the ordinary, that's a special magic, isn't it? You know what that's called, right?"

"A miracle," said Bailey.

"That's right," I said. Just then Sam stepped over to where Bailey was standing and put his foot down in the puddle, splashing his brother.

"Hey!" Bailey exclaimed, as Sam ran off laughing. "Come over here again and I'll be ready for you, Sam," he warned.

"Dad?" said Bailey.

"Yeah, buddy?"

"Do magicians ever make real magic — miracles, I mean?"

"No, I don't think so. They create illusions which look like miracles. They can't really make bunnies appear out of nowhere or saw a woman in half and put her back together again."

"Okay, that's what I thought," said Bailey. "So only God can make miracles?"

"Yes, well, except for when he gives humans or angels the power to do them. But all that power is really God's. He just loans it to people sometimes."

"So how do you know he doesn't loan it to some magicians?"

"Because they always do the same sorts of tricks and they do them just to amuse people. God doesn't do miracles just for entertainment."

"Why not?"

"Because that would be frivolous."

"What's that?"

"Umm ... it means being silly or just goofing off. God does miracles only to help people or maybe to punish some wicked people."

"Oh," said Bailey, as we both stared out at the now-flooded parking lot. "Was Jesus ever friv ... fr — "

"Frivolous?"

"Yeah."

"No, I don't think so. Even when he said funny things, which he did sometimes, it was for some important reason."

"Was it important when he walked on the water?"

"Ooh ... good one, Bailey. That does almost seem like he was doing a magic trick, doesn't it?"

"Yeah."

"Like he was showing off for his disciples."

"Uh huh."

"But do you remember what happened in that story when they saw him walking on the water?"

"They were scared."

"Yes, but then what did one of the disciples do?"

"He walked on the water too."

"Yeah, and then what happened?"

"He sank into the water."

"Right, but then Jesus saved him and taught him a lesson. Do you remember what that was?"

"What?"

"That he needed to trust God and have faith. That was a crucial lesson for that man, Peter, and it's important for us too. So Jesus wasn't just showing off when he walked on water."

The rain began to dissipate, and when it slowed to a drizzle, the boys walked out to the drain and looked into it for a few minutes. Then they went back over to the new play set and played for a while.

As we climbed back on our bikes to head home, Sam asked, "Did God stop the rain, Dad?"

"Yeah, he did," I said.

"That was nice," declared Sam. "I would hate to ride home in the rain."

God is in control of the world. Every Christian would agree with that. But exactly what does that control entail? *There* is where Christians often fiercely disagree. In recent years it has become fashionable in some circles to diminish the degree of God's control over the world, especially when it comes to our lives and the choices we make. Some of these folks — I call them latter-day deists — actually endorse and celebrate the notion that God does not know in advance our future decisions and the remaining course of human history. God takes risks, they say, in the sense that his plan for the world may or may not ultimately succeed, depending on the choices we mortals make. Proponents of this view somehow find it exhilarating. I find it terrifying. But of course, one's emotional response to a doctrine is, in the end, irrelevant. The real issue is whether it is true. So does God take risks? Is he ignorant of our future choices and what remains of human history? Does he lack complete control of the world?

Through the prophet Isaiah the Lord declares, "I make known the end from the beginning" (Isa. 46:10). God backs up this claim with hundreds of predictive prophecies, some pertaining to events thousands of years in the future. The psalmist declares, "All the days ordained for me were written in your book before one of them came to be" (Ps. 139:16). In Proverbs we are told, "In his heart a man plans his course, but the LORD determines his steps" (Prov. 16:9). Such passages don't suggest a God who is ignorant of the future or who takes risks. In fact, Scripture presents us with a portrait of a God in complete control. This is well-emphasized by the writer of Hebrews when he begins his letter by noting that God "sustain[s] all things by his powerful word" (Heb. 1:3), and by Paul when he says, "[Christ] is before all things, and in him all things hold together" (Col 1:17). And Paul writes that God "works out everything in conformity with the purpose of his will" (Eph. 1:11). That sounds like complete control to me and, considering the loving-kindness of God, the most comforting and exhilarating truth possible.[28] This biblical idea that God sustains everything from moment to moment has profound implications. For one thing, it prevents us from lapsing into a virtual deism, the notion that the world somehow runs on its own and that God intervenes only from time to time. In reality, God is intimately involved with every aspect of our lives and closer to us than we can possibly imagine. This doctrine of divine conservation of the world, as it is sometimes called, essentially refutes the thesis of that well-known American philosopher, Bette Midler, who once declared, "God is watching us *from a distance*."[29]

The doctrine of divine conservation enables us to see miracles not as exceptional cases of divine activity in the world but as instances of *unique* divine activity. If God is always acting to preserve the world from moment to moment, then miracles are simply changes in the divine routine. God's regular governance is what we call the laws of nature. His deviations from that routine are what we call miracles. Both the laws of nature and miracles are equally divine communications to us, signs of his sovereignty, though in the case of miracles, his messages are typically more apparent. In Scripture, miracles are often referred to as "signs and wonders."[30] They are God's communication to us, an aspect of divine revelation.

Jesus himself is the ultimate divine revelation, because he is not an inanimate thing but a person, God in the flesh. In Christ, God not only communicates but also connects with us in the deepest existential way. So intimate is that connection that the church — we, his people — are referred to as his body. Think for a moment how close you are to your own body, and the force of this metaphor will hit you afresh. I suppose this is another reason to be confident that we'll know Jesus when we see him.

When Will
We See Jesus?

After an evening of shopping, Sam, Maggie, Andrew, and Amy were enjoying ice cream cones in the van when Sam piped up from the back seat with a question. Trying to carry on a conversation in the van is like trying to converse in a wind tunnel, what with Andrew crying, Maggie chattering away between bites, and They Might Be Giants blaring from the CD player.

"Mom, does God want us to be in heaven?" asked Sam.

"Yes, Sam, he does," Amy answered cheerfully.

"Does that mean that God wants us to die?"

"Dang ... didn't see that coming," Amy muttered to herself. Then, thinking quickly, she replied, "God has a plan for each of us, Sam, and he wants us to be on earth as long as it takes for us to accomplish his plan. Then when we get to heaven, he gives us new bodies, and we live forever. So really we will be more alive in heaven than we are here."

Amy gave herself a mental pat on the back, while Sam's attention turned to the ice cream dripping down his arm. When Amy shared this with me, I congratulated her for being so quick with a theologically orthodox response.

A few days later, Sam, Bailey, and I were out on the front porch shucking corn together when Sam suddenly asked, "Dad, God can do anything, right?"

"Yes, Sam," I said.

"Can he make himself die?"

"No, Sam. God can't do that, because then he wouldn't be God," I declared confidently.[31]

"But Jesus was God, and he died," said Sam.

"Dang," I thought to myself. "Didn't see that coming."

"Well, Sam," I said, clearing my throat, "Jesus' body died, but his soul lived on. And as God, he has always lived."

"Oh," said Sam. "Look at this, Dad. This one's *perfect*." He beamed, holding up a pristine ear of corn. "No stringy things at *all*!"

"Way to go, Sam," I said.

"Dad?" he said.

"Yeah, buddy?"

"When will we see Jesus?"

"Hmm … probably when we die and go to heaven. He'll be waiting for us, and it will be great," I said, handing him an unshucked ear of corn.

"We'll be happy all the time?" he asked.

"Oh yeah," I said.

"And we'll never mess up like we do here," he added.

"That's right. He's going to take away all of our sin and make us perfect as human beings. So we'll always do what's right and never get in any trouble."

"That's hard to imagine," said Bailey.

"I can imagine it," said Sam.

"No, you can't, Sam," Bailey said sternly.

"Yes, I can," Sam shot back.

"No you ca —"

"Guys!" I said. "Don't fight about it. Bailey, if he says he can imagine it, then that's okay."

This settled them down, and we all resumed shucking our corn.

"See, guys," I said after a few moments, "that kind of thing won't happen in heaven. We won't even have little squabbles like you two did just now."

"Because everybody will agree about things?" asked Bailey, tugging on a fistful of husk.

"Probably," I said. "Or if we ever do disagree about something, we'll be patient and find joy in it."

"That's amazing," said Bailey. "So Dad, why are people sad when Christians die?"

"Mainly because we will miss them. Also, we feel sorry for those who loved them who are still alive in this world. We don't feel sorry for Christians when they die. We are happy for them, because they are home. Do you remember how last year those students died in the van accident and how sad we all were?"

"Yeah."

"Everyone was so sad because of what *we* had lost. And we felt especially bad for the moms and dads and siblings of those students, because now they won't see them again until heaven. And for a lot of people that will be a long time from now."

"So it's like they went on a trip, right?" said Sam.

"Who?" Bailey asked.

"The people who died," Sam clarified.

"Yes, that's right. Or you might say that *all* of us Christians are on a trip to see Jesus, and they just arrived ahead of us."

"Do they miss us?" Bailey asked, breaking the stem off an ear of corn.

"You mean, do they feel sad?"

"Uh huh."

"No, they don't feel sad at all, only happy. But I think they look forward to our arrival. It's just one more thing for them to look forward to."

"Dad?" said Sam.

"What, buddy?" I replied, reaching for the last unshucked ear of corn.

"Can we talk to the people in heaven, I mean, to say hi and find out what they are doing?"

"No, I'm afraid not. And, actually, we're not supposed to even try."

"How do you know?" asked Bailey.

"The Bible says we aren't supposed to try to contact people in the next world. That's called the occult and lots of people do it, but it's wrong."[32]

"Then why do they do it if the Bible says not to?"

"Some people don't know the Bible says it's wrong, and other people do know, but they try it anyway, because they want so badly to connect with their loved ones who have died. And some do it because they want to learn about the future."

"How do they do it?"

"Through people called mediums. They practice witchcraft and invite spirits to speak through them. This is not only wrong but very dangerous."

"Why?" Bailey asked, making a final inspection of his clean ear of corn before handing it to me.

"Because there are bad angels who pose as dead friends and relatives, and when people invite them into their lives, they join the side of darkness. Their lives get really messed up and they can't tell right from wrong."

"So they never really get to talk to their friends in heaven?"

"No, at least not usually. They just think they are talking to them."

"That's dumb. They should know it's not really the people in heaven," he declared, squinting his disapproval.

"Well, Bailey, they are fooled because those spirits really can predict the future sometimes."

"Really?"

"Look, let me tell you a story. There was this king of Israel named Saul, and his army was not doing very well, and he was afraid his army would be defeated by the enemy they were about to fight. So Saul went to a witch and asked her to contact the spirit of his dead friend Samuel."[33]

"Hey, that's *my* name!" Sam said.

"That's right, and this Sam was a really good guy like we want you to be." Sam smiled. "Anyway," I continued, "King Saul wanted to consult Samuel about Israel's upcoming battle."

"So what happened?" asked Bailey.

"The witch contacted Samuel, and Samuel told Saul that his army was going to lose to their enemy — and that's exactly what happened."

"So he told the king the future?" asked Bailey.

"Yes, and that's why a lot of people go to mediums and witches, because they want to find out about the future. But it didn't help Saul, did it?"

"No. They still lost."

"So maybe we should just trust God with the future, huh?"

"Definitely," Bailey said as he stood up and brushed himself off.

"We don't know what will happen in our lives — when we'll see Jesus or even if we'll get to eat this corn. But God knows, and that's all that matters. Do you know what it's called when you trust God about the future?"

"What?"

"Faith."

"Oh yeah, I knew that."

"Good, Bailey. Don't forget it."

One of my favorite games to play with the kids is hide-and-seek tag. As you might guess, it is just a hybrid of tag and hide-and-seek. In this game, a base is designated, and the person who is it must tag one of the hiders before they make it back to base. Some hiders don't emerge from their hiding place until they are spotted by the seeker. But others like to try to sprint back to base as soon as they think they have a decent chance of making it there without being tagged. This is one of those areas where the different personalities of Sam and Bailey are apparent. Bailey always waits until he's spotted before racing to base. Sam, on the other hand, likes to take off running as soon as he can, even if it means increasing his chances of being tagged. He just can't stand the suspense.

What I love about hide-and-seek tag is the fact that it combines athletics and drama. You can get a pretty good workout playing the game, and the mystery involved still gives me the same thrilling anxiety I experienced as a kid. A few weeks ago, while playing the game with Bailey and Sam at the park, I suddenly figured out what makes the game so exciting. When Bailey was it, I hid behind a large tree, not far from the base, in hopes that once he walked a few feet away I would enjoy a quick and easy sprint to victory. Unfortunately for me, after he finished counting, Bailey began to walk in my direction. Suddenly I was in a quandary. If I kept peering out from behind the tree, he would likely spot me and I'd be tagged. But if I didn't peek, I'd have no way of knowing where he was, which is terribly nerve-wracking.

This is the wonderful dilemma that makes all hide-and-seek games so much fun: do I take the risk of gathering more information about my situation, or do I take the safer but more suspenseful approach of not peeking? Every turn is different, and the hider must make this assessment anew each time. Bailey and Sam deal with the suspense in different ways, but they both love it. This explains why it is their favorite game and why we've played hundreds of times.

Just as in a game of hide-and-seek, mystery and suspense make life a better drama, a more thrilling adventure. Yes, it can be nerve-wracking not being able to predict what the days ahead will bring, particularly when lives and relationships hang in the balance. Yes, it takes great faith to trust God entirely regarding one's future. But who could be more trustworthy than God? If you can't trust a loving omnipotence, then who can you trust? The biblical prescription is to "cast all your anxiety on [the Lord] because he cares for you" (1 Peter 5:7) and to "trust in the Lord and do good.... Delight yourself in the Lord and he will give you the desires of your heart" (Ps. 37:3–4).

Occult practice is wildly popular in our culture. The tools of that trade—tarot cards, Ouija boards, crystal balls, and the like—are big sellers. And you can find plenty of "professional" fortune-tellers in any city. It always amuses me, though, that their offices tend to be run-down shacks or trailers, which should give pause to any sensible person. If they're so good at telling fortunes, then shouldn't they be making more money, at least enough to put a decent sign out front? Perhaps the really skilled fortune-tellers aren't doing their tricks in those hovels anyway. Maybe they're at the racetrack or in Las Vegas using their psychic skills to rake in the dough.

"No fair peeking!" kids often say. Well, that's also what God says to us regarding most of the future, although some events he has chosen to reveal to us in biblical prophecies. Scripture strongly forbids consulting fortune-tellers and other spiritists,[34] and not just because God doesn't want us to waste our money on them. While many fortune-tellers are frauds, the biggest hazard is when they are not a fraud. For one thing, to dabble in that stuff is to open a portal into a dark and dangerous world, to invite influence by beings both sinister and powerful. On top of this, when it comes to having one's future told, there is really nothing to be gained. Suppose, like King Saul, a person consults a fortune-teller to learn about what lies ahead. If the news is bad, then the person will be filled with dread while waiting for the apparently inevitable painful fate to befall. If the news is good, then the person is robbed of the true thrill of a happy adventure, like a kid peeking at her Christmas presents before Christmas morning. So the person comes away either filled with anxiety or with a spoiled surprise. This is why fortune-telling is not just wrong, it's dumb, as Bailey would put it.

Thankfully, we worship a God who knows everything, including the future. However, it is interesting to note that in the Gospels there appear to be some things that were hidden from Jesus, such as the precise time of his return and the identity of the woman who was healed when she touched his garment.[35] Yet Jesus seemed to know full well how he was to die and even some details that were called to his attention, such as Peter's threefold denial of Christ. Perhaps — and this is a *theory* — Jesus had access to facts about the future, but these things weren't always on his mind. Just as we remember facts and past events when prompted,[36] Jesus possibly had knowledge of the future that he could call to mind. When Peter declared he would never deny him, this was a trigger, prompting Jesus to "remember" the future and offer Peter a prophetic corrective. One wonders how many times Jesus corrected people, especially his disciples, when they made claims about the future. That's the sort of thing that could make a person pretty self-conscious. It could even have the effect of getting a person to follow the advice of the proverb which says, "Do not boast about tomorrow, for you do not know what a day may bring forth" (Prov. 27:1).

By the way, since Jesus does know the future, his knowledge of us, his church, includes our glorified state. He doesn't just know us in our present fallen, struggling, sometimes despairing condition. He is right now fully aware of us in our final, sinless form, perfected in our humanity, our unique beauty in Christ fully realized. Remember the question we considered earlier: why does God love us? Maybe this is one part of the explanation. His love for us is not focused on our present struggles but is geared toward our glorified selves, in which our redemption will culminate. The transforming grace of God will *make* us worthy of his love. Since God transcends time, he is not limited to viewing us as we are right now. From all eternity he has beheld us in our glorified state. That is our wonderful destiny, to which Paul refers when he says, "He chose us in [Christ] before the creation of the world to be holy and blameless in his sight" (Eph. 1:4).

The concept of the glorification of Christians is a crucial aspect to the doctrine of grace. Not only is it stunningly hopeful and inspiring but it explains why we will not be ashamed when we stand before him in heaven. We don't know when we will see Jesus, but we do know that when it happens, we will not only be forgiven, we will be, at last, complete — human as human was meant to be. When we see Jesus, we will be like him in his humanity — fully realized, fully transformed, and fully beautiful. For Christians, this is a peek into the future God has guaranteed us. If you want hope regarding what lies ahead, what else do you need to know?

And yet we do know more about our future hope. Much more, in fact . . .

13

What Will We Do in Heaven?

When we took our family trip last year, we decided to leave our gecko in the hands of our neighbors, the Shutts. Just prior to our departure, Brandy Shutt asked Amy, "What if Toledo dies while you're gone?" Amy facetiously replied, "If that happens, just go buy another gecko to replace him."

Well, guess what? Toledo died while we were gone. When we broke the news to the boys on our way home, their response was, "Can we get another gecko?" No mourning. No stunned disbelief. Not even a moment's silence for good ole Toledo. When we informed the kids that we already had a new gecko waiting for us — the Shutts had dutifully marched right out and purchased another gecko to replace him — the kids immediately began to think of names. Their decision came as quickly as it did the first time. Our new gecko's name would be Mac.

When we first met Mac, he was a fragile little thing with a vision problem. He seemed to have a lazy left eye, or at any rate he could not open it completely. This made for a rather comical sight when we would feed him. Whereas Toledo could spot his prey from the other side of his terrarium, Mac could barely see it when it was directly in front of him. And when he would lunge for the worm or cricket, he would often miss completely. For the first few weeks, we had to dangle his food right in front of his face to get him to eat. It was pitiful, and it made the loss of Toledo that much harder to take — at least for Amy and me. The boys didn't seem to mind. In fact, they laughed at little Mac as he would founder in his attempts to capture his prey. They would point and giggle, and Amy and I would shake our heads in dismay that our new reptile was a pathetic klutz.

We never learned for certain what killed Toledo, but we did find out that it is important to supplement a gecko's diet with calcium, as they tend to suffer from deficiencies of this nutrient. Perhaps our lack of attention to this was what doomed Toledo. In any case, we made sure to provide Mac with calcium, along with a well-balanced diet of crickets and meal worms. Happily, he soon began to thrive; he grew steadily and eventually his left eye began to work properly. He still had difficulty hunting crickets, as he was not as sprightly as his predecessor, but he functioned well enough for our boys to stop laughing at him.

Well, that is until Amy accidentally disfigured the poor lizard.

Molting was difficult for Mac for the first few months, so we would often assist him by pulling the dead skin off his body. While doing this on one occasion, Mac tried to get away, and Amy seized him by the tail. Apparently Mac was especially eager to escape, because he ran off leaving his tail twitching in Amy's hand. She was horrified, but, predictably, the boys were delighted, thinking it was the coolest thing they'd ever seen. Sam was especially excited when he learned that in some rare cases geckos which lose tails sometimes grow back two or more. So again, Mac was the object of laughter for the boys. This time, though, it was not because he was an oaf but because he was a freak.

One day after doing some batting practice with Bailey and Sam, we climbed up into the second story of the fort and sat down to take a breather. We chatted about baseball and a few random topics, then Sam changed the subject.

"Dad, is Toledo in heaven right now?"

"Yes, I think he is."

"What do you think he's doing?" Bailey asked. Sam looked at Bailey then back at me, nodding as if to reinforce his brother's question.

"I'm not sure, but he's having a lot more fun there than he ever had here on earth."

"Animals don't eat each other there, right?" said Bailey.

"Right, the Bible says that the lion will eat straw like an ox. It also says that leopards will lie down with goats. Can you imagine napping with a leopard?"[37]

"I don't think I could sleep," declared Sam, gritting his teeth.

"No way," added Bailey.

"Well, you won't have anything to fear in heaven, because there will be no more pain and sadness."

"We'll be happy all the time?" asked Bailey, as he fidgeted with a baseball.

"Yes," I said. "We won't get sick or grow old."

"Will Mac have a new tail in heaven?" asked Sam.

"Sam," said Bailey, "he's going to get a new tail *before* he gets to heaven. Remember? It's going to grow back."

"Dad," Sam continued, ignoring his brother, "do you think maybe Toledo has *two* tails in heaven?"

"I don't know about that. I just know that all of the animals in heaven will be totally healthy. So will we, because we'll get new bodies that are much stronger and more beautiful than these bodies we have now."[38]

"But *we* won't have tails. People don't grow tails," Sam said.

"Good point," I said, as Bailey rolled his eyes.

"Will we be like superheroes?" Sam asked, his voice rising with excitement.

"Um, well, yeah," I stammered. "Compared to how it is in these bodies, we'll be like superheroes."

"Cool!" exclaimed Sam.

"What will we do there?" said Bailey.

"We'll do a lot of the same things we do here ... maybe even *this*," I said, taking the baseball from Bailey and cocking my arm as if to throw.

"Hey!" said Bailey, grinning.

"Will we play soccer?" asked Sam.

"I think so, and maybe other sports too. We'll also spend our time with people talking and teaching each other things. We'll do a lot of learning, but we won't forget things like we do here. We'll make wonderful art — especially music. And we'll do all of these things in the presence of God. We'll be worshiping him in each activity."

"How many people will be there?" Bailey asked.

"I don't know," I said. "But I expect it will be millions and millions of people."

"Millions?!" said Sam with wide eyes.

"Yeah, and that's just human beings from this planet. Who knows what other kinds of people will be there from other worlds God has made."

"Whoa," said Bailey. "That's kind of scary."

"No, Bailey. That's one thing it definitely will *not* be — scary. Heaven will feel more like home to us than anything we've ever felt in this world. You know how good it feels when you come home from a long trip?"

"Yeah."

"Well, it will be thousands of times more satisfying than that, because heaven is your true home. And you miss it now even though you don't realize it."

"Really?"

"Yes, every time you feel sad or disappointed or just not totally happy, that's because you're longing to be home with Jesus and the millions of wonderful friends you're going to have." Bailey nodded slowly, as I rolled the baseball back to him. Sam stood up and leaned back against the wall of the fort.

"Do you know that the Bible says that God has put eternity in our hearts?"[39]

"What does that mean?" asked Bailey.

"I think it means a lot of things. It probably has something to do with the fact that everyone wants to live forever. I also believe everyone has a sense, deep down inside, that we *can* live forever.[40] But the reason I mentioned that verse just now is because I think it also means that God has given us a sense of our real home in heaven. Don't you have that feeling inside you?"

"Yeah, I think so," said Bailey, shifting the baseball from hand to hand.

"So you know what I'm talking about. Everybody has that feeling, pal."

"Even bad guys?"

"Yes, though they may get to the point where they don't realize it. Remember how we've talked about how sin messes up the way people think?"

"Yeah," said Bailey pensively.

"Well, that applies here. They still desire to go to heaven, but they don't understand that that is what they want."

"Weird."

"But, Bailey, the only reason we understand that heaven is our home is because God has enabled us to. That is his gift just as much as his taking us there. And if we follow Jesus, then he'll do just that. Nothing can keep it from happening. Isn't that great?"

"Uh huh," Bailey said, almost in a whisper. Sam had turned around and was looking out toward the yard, but I could see he was listening intently.

"So one day, just as sure as I'm talking to you now, we'll all be together in heaven, hanging out with wonderful people who worship God just as we do."

"They'll all be our friends, right?" Sam interjected.

"Yes, but they'll be better and closer friends than we've ever known in this world. You guys, think how much fun you have with your friends — Elijah, Conner, and your cousins."

"And Hayden and Jacob," said Bailey.

"Don't forget Noah and Ethan," added Sam, turning around quickly as he spoke.

"Right. Wouldn't it be great if everyone in the *world* were someone you liked that much and who liked you as much as they do?"

"Yeah," Bailey and Sam said, nearly in unison.

"That's how it will be in heaven, only tons better. Nothing but good friends everywhere. Imagine that. Millions of people and each one a good friend."

"That sounds like ... heaven," Bailey said, smiling.

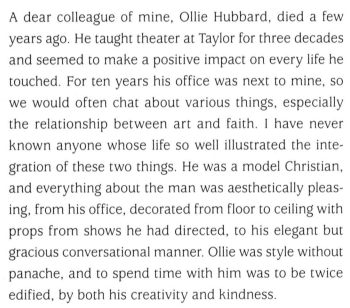

A dear colleague of mine, Ollie Hubbard, died a few years ago. He taught theater at Taylor for three decades and seemed to make a positive impact on every life he touched. For ten years his office was next to mine, so we would often chat about various things, especially the relationship between art and faith. I have never known anyone whose life so well illustrated the integration of these two things. He was a model Christian, and everything about the man was aesthetically pleasing, from his office, decorated from floor to ceiling with props from shows he had directed, to his elegant but gracious conversational manner. Ollie was style without panache, and to spend time with him was to be twice edified, by both his creativity and kindness.

In 2003 Ollie was diagnosed with pancreatic carcinoma, an especially aggressive form of cancer. He made the most of his final months, spending time with his family and getting ready for his imminent demise.

Though he did all he could in preparing to die, Ollie struggled with anxiety about it nearly until the end. In his final hours, with a good friend at his side, Ollie drifted in and out of consciousness. Suddenly, Ollie opened his eyes and declared, "Everything's okay. I've been on the other side." When his friend prodded him for an explanation, Ollie said, "I was in a room with my grandmother, Don Odle, and my favorite dog. It's just fascinating!" Don Odle was a long-time coach at Taylor University and Ollie's friend. But, like Ollie's grandmother and pet dog, Don was deceased. So what was going on here? In any case, after this experience Ollie's anxiety about dying disappeared, and he made his passage into the next world peacefully.

As I have reflected on this story, I've wondered about the significance of the three figures Ollie encountered in that "room." When I first heard this anecdote, the combination struck me as random and peculiar. Then I realized that this small group represents the full range of human relationships — those found with family, friends, and pets. The three also exemplify vocation and recreation, society and nature, and even the roles we play in life as superiors, peers, and inferiors. Perhaps this was one of God's subtle purposes in giving Ollie this experience — not only to encourage him that "fascinating" things lay in store for him but also to communicate the completeness of heaven's bounty.

It is common for people to ask whether there will be animals in heaven. I've always been perplexed by this question because, at the risk of sounding condescending, the answer is obvious. Scripture clearly indicates that animals will be in heaven. The description of the peaceable kingdom in Isaiah includes several references to animals. And in the book of Revelation John declares that "every creature in heaven and on earth" sings praises to God (Rev. 5:13). Also, in that book (Rev. 4:6 – 10; 5:14; 7:11) are repeated references to some special animals who give glory and honor to God. This is easy to overlook, however, because the Greek word *zoon* used in these passages is usually translated as "creature" and sometimes as "beast" (KJV and Wycliffe). *Zoon* is, in fact, equivalent to our English "animal."

But do animals have souls? While I don't think this question is decisive regarding whether there will be animals in heaven, it is worth noting that a Hebrew term for soul (*nephesh*) is used for both man and animals by the writer of Ecclesiastes, when he asks, "Who knows if the spirit of man rises upward and if the spirit of the animal goes down into the earth?" (Eccl. 3:21). There is also a bit of linguistic irony in the question of whether animals have souls, since the Latin root of *animal* is *anima*, which *means* "soul."

Another reason to be confident that animals will be in heaven is the fact that animals are an important part of our life here on earth. Our fellowship with our pets is one of life's sweetest experiences, and even for those who don't have pets, the experience of animals in nature can be deeply moving. Animals are beautiful, sometimes awesomely so, and reflect the glory of God in many ways. So why would God withhold such a good thing in the next world? Why would God make heaven deficient in this regard?

When Paul says that "the creation waits in eager expectation for the sons of God to be revealed" (Rom. 8:19) and that "the whole creation has been groaning as in the pains of childbirth" for our final redemption (Rom. 8:22), this includes animals. Though they do not bear the image of God, animals have struggled with us and, well, because of us. That animals will take part in God's eternal kingdom will make it that much more beautiful.

Former president of Taylor University, Jay Kesler, had a dying friend named Jim, who was an associate pastor of a church. Jay and another friend went to visit him in the hospital, but it appeared to be too late, as Jim had slipped into a coma the day before, and it appeared he would never awaken. But they went in to see Jim anyway, and as soon as they opened the door, Jim greeted them. "You guys, everything's okay. It's *real*. They said

I could come back and talk to you two before I go." "They," Jim explained, were angels with whom he had been conversing and singing hymns. He was exploding with excitement about it, and the three of them prayed together. When it was Jim's turn, he said, "Lord, these guys clearly don't understand the things I've seen. But that's okay. Please take care of them." Shortly after this, Jim said, "I'm tired. I've gotta go," and he passed away.

Heaven will be a busy place, full of blessed activity. We will feast at a banquet (Isa. 25:6; Matt. 8:11; Luke 13:29). We will laugh, sing, and praise God (Luke 6:21 – 23; Isa. 6:3; Rev. 4:8). We will fellowship with a variety of people (Rev. 5:9; 7:9) and hang out with Jesus (John 14:2 – 3; Rev. 22:4). We will behold a temple of God (Rev. 11:19; 15:5) and there will be an enormous city (Rev. 21:15ff; Heb. 11:16). We will serve God (Rev. 7:15; 22:3) and enjoy rest (Rev. 14:13). And all of this we will do while dwelling in new, imperishable bodies (1 Cor. 15:42).

What this means is that the next world will be a *lot* like our present life on earth, with eating, friendship, laughter, music, celebration, animals, water, trees, fruit, architecture, and a city with gates and streets. But the next world will be very different, insofar as there will be no more pain or sorrow (Isa. 25:8; Rev. 21:4) but only joy and pleasure (Ps. 16:11). Most important, God will be worshiped by all (Phil. 2:10; Rom. 14:11).

In popular culture heaven is parodied so much that it is possible even for Christians to become a bit fuzzy regarding what it is all about. The cartoon version of heaven varies in certain respects. Sometimes it's people sitting on fluffy clouds playing harps. Or it might be a robed St. Peter checking off names at the pearly gates. Or a rendering of God as an old man with a long, flowing beard. But the one constant among them is the depiction of heaven as colorless, formless, and bland. Whatever goes on there, we are told, heaven is boring, not the kind of place any reasonable person would want to visit, much less inhabit for eternity.[41]

I wonder if it is sheer accident that this stereotype of heaven is precisely opposite the biblical truth. Heaven is not an ethereal, abstract realm but a world more real and substantial than that in which we now dwell. It is not a vacuous, colorless expanse but a sensory delight, rich in colors, sounds, tastes, smells, and textures that our fallen imaginations cannot begin to fathom. It is not populated by blasé ticket-takers but an ebullient community of like-minded people, united in a common love of God and for one another. Heaven is not a bleached-out version of your local bureau of motor vehicles but the glorious culmination of God's work on earth, all too wondrous for words. There is nothing at all mundane in or about heaven. The place will be overrun with pleasure and excitement.

14

Who Gets to Go to Heaven?

Bailey sat quietly in the back seat, scanning the endless cornfields on Highway 26, holding his baseball hat in his lap. Peeking at him in my rearview mirror, I could see a question forming.

"Dad, do you ever wonder if you will go to heaven?" he asked.

"I used to, but I don't so much anymore. Why?"

"Oh, I was just thinking about it," he said, swiping a bug off his knee with his hat.

"Bailey, do *you* ever wonder if *you'll* go to heaven?"

"Yeah, sometimes."

"How come?"

"I mean ... what if God forgets me or doesn't want me there?"

"Well, let's talk about that," I said. "If God forgot you, do you know what would happen?"

"No, what?" he said, now looking at me.

"You would disappear."

"Why?"

"Because his thinking about you is the only reason you keep existing."

"What does that mean?"

"The Bible says God keeps everything in existence. He preserves you from moment to moment by thinking about you. The only reason you are here at all is because you are on God's mind. If he did forget about you, even for a moment, then *poof*, you'd be gone. So do you know what that means?"

"What?"

"It means that ever since God made you in Mommy's tummy, he has not stopped thinking about you. And that's true for me too, and Mommy and all the other billions of people alive today. We keep existing because God is paying attention to us. Now do you think that God could forget about someone he has thought about so much?"

"No," he replied and pursed his lips.

"Besides, Bailey, God *can't* forget about anything because he's perfect. He knows everything and has a perfect memory. He won't forget you because he can't forget you. You're *unforgettable*, Bailey," I said smiling into the rearview mirror. He fought back an embarrassed grin and looked out the window again.

"Dad?" Bailey said after a few moments of silence. I braced myself for another heavy question.

"Yeah, buddy?"

"Why is there so much corn in Indiana?"

When I was a child I had a terrible fear of being abandoned. My parents were very loving and nurturing, but I still lived with a deep anxiety about being left alone. Once a week they would go out bowling and leave me with one of my older brothers, and watching my mom and dad drive away was devastating. It felt like they were never coming back. No matter what they or my brothers said to reassure me, I felt certain I'd never see them again.

Some people have abandonment fears when it comes to God. And even some of the biblical writers worried that God was snoozing on the job. One of the psalmists writes, "Awake, O Lord! Why do you sleep? Rouse yourself! Do not reject us forever. Why do you hide your face and forget our misery and oppression?" (Ps. 44:23–24). Even the Son of God himself felt this way, as he hung on the cross, quoting another psalmist: "My God, my God, why have you forsaken me?" (Matt. 27:46). Everyone has felt this way at some time or another, perhaps even when not being oppressed. Sometimes it's just a vague sense of aimlessness or wandering. Whatever the case, one may feel forgotten by God. However, God knows our feelings and says in response, "Can a mother forget the baby at her breast and have no compassion on the child she has borne? Though she may forget, I will not forget you!" (Isa. 49:15). The love of God is intensely maternal — comforting and empathetic. God not only governs the whole universe, he tenderly nurtures the least among us, guiding us along our path, drawing us to himself.

But let's face it: sometimes it is hard to believe in God's attentiveness. As the prophet Isaiah says, "Truly you are a God who hides himself" (Isa. 45:15). God could easily make himself quite apparent to us all day long, providing visions, healings, burning bushes, talking donkeys, chariots of fire, voices from the clouds, and other unmistakable signs of his presence. But he doesn't. In fact, today those sorts of miracles seem pretty rare. So where does that leave us?

Faith. What is faith? As children of the Enlightenment, it's tempting to conceive of faith in strictly cognitive terms, as mere belief or intellectual assent. But that's not the biblical perspective. In fact, the book of James says that demons believe ... and shudder (James 2:19). It is instructive to consider that no one has a more orthodox theology than Satan. He knows the truth and believes the right things about God, but his actions and attitude toward the truth are, well, problematic. The Devil is sobering proof that mere true beliefs about God aren't sufficient for salvation.

In Scripture genuine "saving" faith is consistently linked with behavior: obedience, good deeds, a righteous lifestyle (e.g., Isa. 30:15; Gal. 5:22 – 23; James 2:24). And just as frequently, we are told that some are disqualified from salvation because of their disobedience (e.g., Gal. 5:19 – 21; 2 Thess. 1:8; Heb. 4:6).

The relationship between faith and good works has been a source of controversy in the church over the centuries. Some emphasize faith over works because of the worry that people will think that salvation is earned by us rather than a gift of grace. Others emphasize works because of the concern that a sole focus on faith will breed moral laziness. Most Christians agree that there must be balance, and it seems to me that the key in achieving that balance is a high view of God's providence. To recognize that our faith and our works are alike gifts from him will keep us from falling into either of these extremes of legalism or moral laziness.

Faith and good works alike are properly viewed as evidences of God's grace, not as triggering mechanisms for divine favor. If there were anything we could do to cause him to favor us, even if it were a simple act of trust or "accepting Christ," then ours would be a religion of works. Rather, all good works on our part, including our trusting Christ, are but outward manifestations of the inner working of the Spirit.

For our family morning devotion recently we read these verses from Psalm 103:

The LORD is compassionate and gracious,
  slow to anger, abounding in love.
He will not always accuse,
  nor will he harbor his anger forever;
he does not treat us as our sins deserve
  or repay us according to our iniquities.
For as high as the heavens are above the earth,
  so great is his love for those who fear him;
as far as the east is from the west,
  so far has he removed our transgressions from us.

—verses 8–12

This passage wonderfully expresses God's mercy and is as hopeful as anything in Scripture. But when I asked Bailey and Sam what they thought about this passage, Bailey said, "Dad, sometimes I'm afraid I might go to hell."

"Really? Why?" I replied.

"I dunno," he said, suddenly embarrassed.

"Do you think that what Jesus did wasn't enough to save you?" I continued.

"No ... but ... what if I never was a Christian in the first place?" Bailey squeezed a pillow tightly to himself as he spoke.

"Bailey," I said, "if you follow Jesus and do what he says, that is just what it means to be a Christian."

"That's right," said Amy. "Nothing can pluck us from God's hand, because he put us there in the first place. He won't let us go. And what Dad says is true."

"What did Dad say?" Bailey said, cocking his head.

"I said that you need to follow Jesus as well as you can."

"Hmm." Bailey pondered this for a few moments, then shifted gears. "Dad, what if someone never heard of Jesus? Or what if they believe lots of wrong things?"

"Well," I said, "there are people who haven't heard of Jesus who still go to heaven through him. People like Moses and David in the Old Testament never heard of Jesus, but they are in heaven. And people who live in places today where no one knows about Jesus — God can save them through Jesus. Because God can save anyone he wants to. But the only way to be saved is through Jesus, whether or not a person actually hears about him. But they will always show signs of being God's child by following him as well they know how."

"That's what we are doing too," added Amy, "just trying to follow him the best we know how. Also, we need to remember that God's love for us is great."

"It's as high as a mountain!" Sam interjected, reaching toward the ceiling with both hands.

"That's right, and he has removed our sin as far as the east is from the west," I said.

"That's as far as from here to China," said Amy.

"Actually, more like India," said Bailey, putting his index finger to his chin.

"What?" said Amy.

"My teacher said India is farther away."

"Okay," I said, "then India it is."

One of the oldest questions posed to Christian apologists is, What is the fate of those who have never heard the gospel? It long baffled me that this is even a problem for people. After all, God can save anyone he wants to. Then it occurred to me where the question was coming from. It derives from that pesky concept of faith as just a mental state about Jesus Christ. Now, it is certainly important that we teach people about Jesus, since learning about and from him is the only way to become a mature disciple. But those who insist that those who never heard about him can't be saved are inconsistent and unbiblical. For one thing, Abraham, Moses, David, Elijah, and other Old Testament saints were saved, though they had never heard of Jesus. Moreover, I've never met a Christian who believes that all fetuses and infants who die must go to hell. But if fetuses and infants can be saved, then belief in Jesus Christ must not be necessary for salvation. So whatever must be necessary for saving faith, it can't be belief in Jesus.

Some insist that God works differently now than he did in the Old Testament. This approach is problematic for several reasons. First, the view that God works differently now than he did in Old Testament times provides no help in the case of deceased fetuses and infants. Second, to make time a decisive factor implies that God is temporally bound. But it is clear from Scripture that God created time and so cannot be limited by it (see 1 Cor. 2:7; 2 Tim. 1:9; and Titus 1:2). Finally, this approach makes time a decisive factor for God's granting a reprieve to those without explicit faith, while space is not a relevant factor. That is, the Old Testament saints were separated by time from explicit awareness of Jesus, while many people today are separated by space from knowing about him — they were never at the right place to hear the gospel preached. If God can have mercy on the former, then why not the latter?

One lesson here is that we must reject the narrow concept of explicit faith as necessary for salvation. We must recognize what some call *implicit* faith, which is the disposition to trust God, as demonstrated in one's earnestly following God as much as one can, relative to one's understanding of him. This more relaxed concept of saving faith is further recommended by the fact that faith and the good works that follow are graciously bestowed by God. So if God works to redeem a person, then the outward signs of that inner work will vary depending on how much the person knows about who is working in his heart. While it may typically be such that those who are saved by God do come to have explicit faith, it doesn't follow that it *always* works this way.

So who gets to go to heaven? Anyone whom God pleases to take there. As he tells us, "I will have mercy on whom I will have mercy, and I will have compassion on whom I will have compassion" (Exod. 33:19). How do we know who those people are? Though sometimes it's hard to tell, it is those who demonstrate a saving faith in Jesus Christ, whether explicit or implicit, and where faith is understood in the robust biblical sense of proving one's love for God by doing good works. (See 1 John 2:3–6.)

So we can be confident in our salvation, as we obey God and his Spirit moves in our lives. In addition to this, God assures us inwardly, testifying quietly to our hearts that we are his children. As Paul says, we who believe have been "marked in him with a seal, the promised Holy Spirit, who is a deposit guaranteeing our inheritance until the redemption of those who are God's possession" (Eph. 1:13–14). What blessed comfort!

15

If Heaven's So Great, Why Am I Afraid to Die?

ome days are so busy that even the kids are eager to get to bed. This particular Friday was certainly one of those: a birthday party for Bailey's friend Conner at Chuck E. Cheese's, several hours of messy play in the back yard, grocery shopping with Mom, and helping Dad with yard work. So we were all whipped and ready for a good night's sleep.

At bedtime we shared our "favorite things" for the day and took turns praying. Sam was not his usual restless self during prayer time, so I knew he'd conk out quickly. But Bailey's prayer was unusually lengthy and heartfelt. After we finished, Amy kissed the boys goodnight and went downstairs.

I was walking out of the boys' bedroom when I heard Bailey say, "Dad, is tomorrow church day?"

"No, tomorrow's Saturday," I replied, stepping back into the doorway. "The day after that is church day.

Tomorrow I make pancakes for you guys and we let Mommy sleep in."

"Oh yeah. Can we have chocolate chips?"

"Yes, I'll put chocolate chips in the pancakes."

"How many?"

"Plenty."

"Ten?"

"Five or six per pancake."

"Why not ten?"

"I don't want you to have too much sugar."

"Is sugar bad?"

"Too much of it is."

"Should you not give us any sugar?"

"No, a little bit of sugar is okay."

"I love chocolate chips."

"So do I."

"Can we have food coloring too?"

"Not if you have chocolate chips. Remember, you can have one or the other in your pancakes, but not both."

"Why not both? You did both before."

"I know, but it's too much trouble."

"I guess I'll have chocolate chips."

"Good, then that's what we'll do."

Bailey lay there with his hands folded behind his head, and somehow he looked older all of a sudden. His eyes searched the ceiling.

"Dad?"

"Yeah, Bailey?"

"Those students who died in the accident . . ."

"Yeah?" I walked to his bedside.

"They're in heaven now, right?"

"Right."

"We'll see them there?"

"Oh yeah, Bailey. It'll be great. You'll get to meet all of them, and I know that you'll especially like one of them, because he liked to think about all the things we talk about."

"Like God and how to be a good man?"

"Yeah. He also liked to be silly sometimes and goof around. You guys can wrestle and stuff." Bailey nodded, but he didn't smile.

"Gram and Gramps will be there too?"

"Yes, and Mommy and me and all of your friends." Now I could see his face tighten and his eyes begin to pool with tears.

"What's wrong, buddy?"

"I just . . . feel bad." Bailey rolled to his side and wiped his hand over his eyes.

"Why?"

"I don't want to tell you."

"Why not?"

"I'm afraid you'll be mad."

"Aw, buddy. Is it something you did wrong?" I sat down on Bailey's bed and put my hand on his shoulder.

"No — I mean, I don't think so."

"Then don't worry about making me mad. Just tell me why you feel bad."

"Well, I know heaven is great and all, and that all my friends will be there, and you and Mommy will be there. But . . . I'm scared."

"You're afraid to die?"

Bailey rolled his head back around and looked directly into my eyes.

"Yeah."

"Oh, that's okay, Bailey. It's natural to be afraid to die."

"But heaven is so wonderful and I'm scared of it. So I feel like that makes God sad." He put both hands over his face and began to cry harder.

"Hey, buddy. You're not making God sad." I rubbed his shoulder and patted his back for a few moments. "And anyway, it's not heaven itself that you're afraid of, right?"

After wiping his face, he looked at me again. "Yeah . . . I mean, no. Well, sorta."

"I think there are two things here we need to separate — dying and heaven. You are afraid to die, right?"

"Yeah."

"That's normal, and it's okay."

"Really?"

"Sure."

"But God wants us to die so we can go to heaven."

"Yes."

"So why should we be afraid of that?"

"It's not the going to heaven part we fear. It's the *getting dead* part." Bailey's lips began to crack into a smile, but he caught himself. "I mean, it takes something severe to kill us, doesn't it?"

"What do you mean?"

"God made us so that we don't die too easily. A guy doesn't say, 'I think I'll die now. See you guys later in heaven,' and then close his eyes and die just like that. Right?"

"No." Now Bailey was having a hard time fighting his smile. He put his hands to his mouth to keep from grinning.

"It takes something painful to kill us — like a disease or a car accident."

"Why?"

"That's just how God made our bodies. They don't die easily. Animals too. Remember *Born Free*?"

"Uh huh."

"Remember how Elsa was attacked by that other lion and even went days without food, but she didn't die?"

"Yeah."

"That's because she was tough, and she had a strong will to live."

"But she didn't know about heaven."

"Right, well, my point is that she didn't die easily."

"Is Elsa alive now, Dad?"

"Um, no — probably not."

"How did she die?"

"I don't know."

"Then how do you know she's dead?"

"Because that was forty years ago."

"How long do lions live?"

"Um, I don't know — maybe fifteen or twenty years. Look, the point is that something killed her, but it took a lot to kill her and the dying process *hurt*."

Bailey nodded.

"I think *that* is what you really fear. You're afraid of how much it will hurt when you die."

"Is that wrong?"

"No, it's okay. In fact, it's good." I leaned back toward the foot of Bailey's bed and propped my chin on my palm.

"Why?"

"Because it means we'll work hard to stay alive."

"Does God like that?"

"Yes, he gave us life and gave us jobs to do down here. So it pleases him when we take care of ourselves and do those jobs."

"But he wants us to go to heaven too, right?"

"Yes."

"Would he be mad if we finished all our jobs then killed ourselves?"

"Yes, that would make him mad."

"But why, if we finished all our jobs?"

I sat up straight again to ponder this one. Then I replied, "Bailey, if we are still alive, then we know we have more work to do."

"What do you mean?"

"If we're still alive, it's because God is keeping us alive. And he wouldn't keep us alive if he didn't have a good reason to do so."

"But what about Grandpa? At the end of his life, he was just lying in a bed and couldn't do anything."

"Oh Bailey, he was doing a lot."

"Like what?"

"Like getting to know you and learning about God."

"But those aren't jobs," Bailey said, with a quizzical expression.

"When I say God gave us 'jobs' to do, I don't mean just things like cleaning and building stuff and fixing things. Our jobs also include other ways of helping people, like how you and I are helping each other right now."

"We're helping each other now?"

"Yes, we're learning things together right this moment by talking about God and people and heaven. Anytime you learn something or teach someone or do something helpful, even if it is just by saying a kind word, you are doing your job in this life." I patted Bailey's leg for emphasis as I spoke.

"So Grandpa was doing his job when he was lying on that bed with all the tubes in his nose?"

"Yes, Bailey, that's exactly right. He was put on earth to do thousands of things, and that included marrying my mom and raising my brothers and me and all the little details that involved. And many of the things God gave him to do, my dad wasn't even aware of. In the same way, God has put me here, with you and Mom and your brothers and sister and my job at work. But there are also a ton of other things that I have no idea about which God has prepared for me to do. And if at the end of my life it seems like I'm not doing any good being alive, you can be sure that's not true. God will be using me to do some good. So we can do our jobs and not even know it."

"Like Andrew?"

"Yes, that's a great example. He's just a baby, so he has no idea what joy he brings to our family."

"He's doing his job, right Dad?"

"Yes! That's good, pal."

Bailey and I sat there quietly for a few moments. He rolled over again, resting his face on his hands and staring over at Sam, who was sleeping soundly. A faint smile appeared on Bailey's face, then just as quickly it vanished.

"Dad, even if it didn't hurt to die, I think I might still be scared."

"Hmm. Okay, let's talk about that. So if you knew that you could go to heaven right now and that it wouldn't hurt at all, and God told you it was okay to go, would you go?"

Bailey looked at me and said, "I don't think I would. Is that bad?"

"No, I don't think that's a bad thing. But why wouldn't you go?"

"I guess ... I guess cuz I'd miss you and Mom and Sam and my friends."

"Okay, good. But then what if you knew that your family and your friends were going to be there? Would you go then?"

"Um ... I guess."

"But you're not sure."

"Yeah."

"Why aren't you sure?"

"I don't know." Bailey started to tear up again.

"Hey, buddy, it's okay. You're just like everyone else when it comes to this." I stroked Bailey's head with my hand. "All of us are a little bit scared of the idea of heaven, even though it's a wonderful place."

"Why?"

"Because we've never been there before. It's strange and unknown to us. Let me ask you a question. Would you rather go to Dollywood or Cedar Point?"

"What's Cedar Point?"

"It's an amazing theme park, and it has a lot more rides and attractions than Dollywood. If you could go to either place right now, where would you choose to go?"

"Probably Dollywood."

"And why would you choose Dollywood?"

"Because I like it," he said with a broad smile.

"And because you've been there before, but you haven't been to Cedar Point, right?"

"Right."

"But don't you trust me when I tell you that Cedar Point is great and even more fun than Dollywood?"

"Well, sort of."

"What do you mean 'sort of'?"

"It's just different."

"It's different because you'd rather see it for yourself and then decide?"

"Yeah."

"Okay, then. That's kind of what it's like with heaven. God tells us it's going to be great, and we trust him ... *sort of.*" As I said this, I leaned into Bailey's face, and he giggled. "But you know, we'd really like to see it for ourselves, wouldn't we?"

"Yeah."

"That's how it is with a lot of things, Bailey. We'd rather go with what is familiar than try something new. We prefer food and clothes and toys and even people that we know to those we don't know."

"Mm hmm."

"And we even fear things just because we don't know them."

"What do you mean?"

I paused and looked away for a moment, struggling for an analogy. "Bailey, look at your closet over there. Would you like to walk in there right now without turning on the light?"

"No way."

"Why not?"

"Because I'd be scared," he said, glancing at the dark doorway on the other side of the room.

"Why—because you know there's a tiger or giant spider in there that would attack you?"

"No."

"Then why would you be scared?"

"Because it's dark."

"And why does the darkness frighten you?"

"Because I can't see what's *in* there."

"Exactly. We fear darkness not because of what we know is there but because of what we *don't* know is there."

Bailey wrinkled his brow. "That's weird," he said.

"Yeah, but it's true, isn't it?"

"Yeah, I guess," he said with a crooked grin.

"So maybe the reason you're afraid to go to heaven is because it's so unknown. But I promise you that when you get there, it will all seem familiar and it won't be scary at all."

He nodded slowly.

"In fact, Bailey, it will feel like home—more like home than you've ever felt."

"Wow."

"'Wow' is right."

"But it's okay if I don't want to die yet?"

"Yes, Bailey, that's fine. I don't want to die yet either. We've got a lot of things to do around here, don't we?"

"Yeah," he smiled and squirmed, as I gripped his shoulder, tickling him.

"Like make pancakes and play in the fort and stuff, right?" I said, standing up.

"Right!"

"Okay, you go to sleep and maybe, just maybe, I'll let you have ten chocolate chips in your pancakes tomorrow morning."

"Are you serious?"

"Yes ... *maybe*," I said with mock sternness.

"And food coloring too?"

"Don't push it, buster."

Bailey smiled, pulling the covers tightly around his little body. And as I walked down the stairs, I thought how cool a green chocolate-chip pancake would look.

Every Christian believes in heaven. But how many of us consistently prove this conviction by the way we live? It is so easy to become preoccupied with our earthly concerns, the urgencies and trivialities of everyday life, that we can forget what all of this is pointing to: living forever in a perfect world. Moses once said that if we're strong enough, we live seventy or eighty years, and "their span is but trouble and sorrow, for they quickly pass, and we fly away" (Ps. 90:10). And James says, "What is your life? You are a mist that appears for a little while and then vanishes" (James 4:14). In the ocean of eternity, our lives are an infinitesimally small drop. Yet we are still inclined to cling to this life as if it was all we had. This is understandable for atheists or even agnostics, because they don't believe in an afterlife. But we Christians know this world is passing away and life here is only the beginning. Yet often it takes sickness and death in our midst to remind us that this earthly life is not the end-all but merely a preface — a significant and decisive preface — to an everlasting story.

So why am I afraid to die? Why, though my hope is in heaven, do I sometimes betray this hope by despairing over earthly losses? I've searched my soul about this for many years, and I suspect there are two key factors involved. One of these is the innate will to live. Unlike animals, human beings are not generally creatures of instinct, but one instinct we do have is self-preservation. The extremes to which some people have gone to survive, such as during the Nazi Holocaust, demonstrate how strong this impulse is.

Christians know that to die in this body is to live in the next world. So facing our departure from this world should not contradict our will to live, right? Well, the trouble is — and this is the other key factor — we have not yet seen the next world. We have experienced only this world. In terms of sensory awareness, this earthly realm is all we've known. To have hope in heaven, we must take someone else's word for it. And, if we are honest with ourselves, that's not something any of us is entirely comfortable with.

There are many good reasons to believe and live as a Christian. I've already talked about some of these. In fact, I'd say the case for Christianity, from a logical standpoint, is overwhelming. The philosophical evidence for God, the manuscript evidence for the authority of Scripture, the historical evidence for the resurrection of Christ — all of it is formidable. But however much rational confidence those things may give me, they are cold comfort in the face of my own demise or when trying to encourage someone else who is walking in death's valley. So where is our comfort in death? Not in the *facts* of the Christian worldview but in the *person* of Jesus Christ, who conquered death for us. Paul speaks to this when he writes that Jesus shared in our "humanity so that by his death he might destroy him who holds the power of death — that is, the devil — and free those who all their lives were held in slavery by their fear of death" (Heb. 2:14 – 15).

If we are confident that God will not forget us, that he really will take us to heaven when we leave this world, then whatever fear of death remains in us must have to do with the unknown — or, to put it more harshly, our ignorance about heaven. Scripture has much to say about what awaits us in the next world, but this won't help us unless we meditate on these promises. Doing so will build our hope and motivate us to follow Christ more faithfully. Then, hopefully, we will be not so much afraid of the dark as we are drawn to the light.

16

What If I Sin in Heaven?

Sam's introduction to baseball was the day he stepped face-first into the path of a Louisville Slugger. Evidently, Bailey didn't notice his little brother behind him while he was taking some warm-up swings. I was in the house when Sam came through the door, both hands over his mouth and dripping with blood. Bailey came in right behind him, frantically explaining what had happened. I washed off Sam's face and prepared an ice pack as quickly as I could. After the bleeding stopped, Amy and I surveyed the damage. One of his teeth had been knocked out, and his top two front teeth were cracked and loose.

These were Sam's baby teeth, but since he was three years old at the time, we didn't relish the idea of his being toothless for two years. Thankfully, when we took him to the dentist the next day, the report was not as dismal as we expected. The crack in one of the teeth was not very deep, so he would likely hold on to that one for a while. As for the other, which appeared to be hanging by a thread, the news was not so good. The dentist told us that it would likely die in just a few months. Well, at the time of this writing, it's been over a year since that accident, and that tooth is still holding on, to the amazement of the dentist. Now Sam is five years old, and there's a strong chance it will stay in until his adult tooth replaces it. Amy and I often comment how that tooth typifies Sam himself — tenacious. Not once did Sam whine or complain about his injury. Amy and I sometimes note how we could all learn a lesson from Sam when it comes to dealing with adversity.

One Saturday morning I was working on our front porch steps, stripping and scraping off some old adhesive that remained after I had pulled up some corroded outdoor carpet. The plan was to paint the steps once I could make the surface sufficiently smooth. This job was taking a lot longer than I had anticipated, so I was getting Bailey to help me with it. He is always happy to do an odd job for an extra dollar or two. But he soon found out just how difficult this work is, which probably explains the nature of the theological conversation that commenced.

"What is hell like, Dad?" Bailey asked, as he swept some of the scrapings into a grocery bag.

"It's really bad, son. I don't think we could understand how bad it is."

"What makes it so bad?"

"It's painful. The Bible compares it to being on fire. But the people there are also really sad."

"So they hurt and are sad at the same time?"

"Exactly."

"Why?"

"Because God is punishing them, and they regret that they didn't ask for forgiveness and worship him with their lives." I put some debris in the bag and handed Bailey a scraper.

"How long do they stay like that?"

"Until God finishes punishing them. The Bible says God destroys the wicked."[42]

"That's really sad," said Bailey, as he sat down on the top porch step and began scraping off adhesive.

"You're right," I said. "It's the saddest thing in the world."

"Dad?"

"Yeah, buddy?"

"When we get to heaven, we won't have to worry about hell anymore, right?"

"Right, but actually we don't have to worry about it now, since we follow Jesus."

"No, I mean ... what happens if I sin in heaven?"

"Ohhh, I see," I said, as I stood and leaned on the railing. "Bailey, you don't need to worry about that."

"Why not?"

"Because God will make sure that won't happen."

Bailey stopped his scraping and looked at me. "How?"

"Remember how we've talked about original sin?"

"Uh huh."

"And how we have a natural tendency to be selfish and disobey God?"

"Right."

"In heaven God takes all that away. He makes us perfect human beings who always want to please God and worship him with our lives."

"Wow — so we'll never *want* to sin because we won't be selfish anymore?" Bailey squinted at the thought of this.

"I know it's hard to imagine, since all we've ever known is how we want to do things our own way."

"But God can do things we can't imagine."

"That's exactly right."

"But Dad," Bailey continued, his expression turning very serious, "if God can make it so we don't sin in heaven, then why doesn't he do that now?"

"That sure would save us a lot of pain and sadness, wouldn't it?" I said, sensing that I was getting in over my head. At this moment I would have preferred to be in a classroom dealing with my students' questions.

"Yeah. So why doesn't he just stop it all right now?"

"Well, I think it's because he wants to use it to make us better."

"What do you mean?"

"I mean that when bad things happen to us, we can grow and become better as a result."

"How?"

"Um ... well, take for example when somebody is mean to you. That gives you an opportunity to forgive them, right?"

"Yeah."

"And it's good to forgive, right?"

"Uh huh."

"So by having that experience, you grow and become more like Jesus. Or what if someone is drowning and another person has to risk his own life to save him? That takes courage, doesn't it?"

"I guess. It depends on where the person is drowning."

"Okay, suppose the person is drowning in a fast-flowing river where there are lots of jagged rocks."

"Yeah, *that* would be scary," he said, pointing for emphasis.

"And it would take courage to jump in and help, wouldn't it?"

"Oh yeah. I couldn't do it."

"I wouldn't want you to since you're still a kid. But when you're a grown man, I hope you would do it."

"I hope so too."

"At any rate, if God took away all the bad things in this world, then he would also be taking away some really good things, like forgiveness and courage."

"Why?"

"Remember, Bailey — because you can't forgive unless somebody did something to hurt you. And you can't have courage unless there is danger."

"Oh, I get it. We get better that way, right?" Bailey said, flicking a bug off one of the steps.

"Exactly. It's better to be forgiving and courageous than not to have those traits. And there are other ways we can grow by dealing with painful experiences."

"Like what?"

"Like patience. You know how hard it is to wait for Maggie when she's taking a long time to put on her shoes?"

"Yeah, I can't stand that."

"Well, that's helping you to become more patient. Or when you accidentally hit Sam in the teeth with that bat."

"Dad, I don't like talking about that."

"But it will help you to understand this. You were sad when Sam got hurt like that, weren't you, even though it was an accident?"

"Yeah."

"Do you know what that's called?"

"What?"

"Sympathy."

"Is that good?"

"Yeah, Bailey, it's really good. And just like those other things — patience, forgiveness, and courage — it is a quality that Jesus had. Jesus is patient, courageous, sympathetic, and forgiving, and that's what makes him so great. So when we develop those qualities, we become more like Jesus. Isn't that wonderful?"

"Yeah, that's cool." Bailey sat silently for a few moments, picking at some of the loose pieces of adhesive on one of the porch steps.

"Dad?"

"What, buddy?"

"Is that like gum?"

"How do you mean?"

"You have to chew gum really hard before you can make a bubble."

"Yes, Bailey! That's a fantastic analogy. I'm impressed." Bailey smiled and made a thumbs up.

"But you know what else it's like, Bailey?"

"What?"

"It's like this porch. It takes a lot of pain to get these steps to look beautiful."

"That's for sure."

"So let's get back at it," I said, as I sat down and resumed chipping away at the adhesive.

"Aw, Dad," said Bailey.

"C'mon, buddy," I said, "let's make these steps beautiful."

God is in the business of redemption. As I discussed earlier, he brings good out of bad situations and sanctifies us through our trials. In fact, this seems to be his primary method of forming our character. But what is most amazing is that the Son of God grew in the same way. The writer of Hebrews says that Jesus "learned obedience from what he suffered" (Heb. 5:8). What? He was already sinless, yet the writer goes on to say that "once made perfect, he became the source of eternal salvation for all who obey him."[43] So even the God-man was perfected through suffering. How much more so, then, do you and I need to suffer in order to be perfected? Think about this as you consider your own trials.

God is making us ready for heaven, and this calls for radical preparation. Though it is tempting to resent our pain and difficulties or even become angry with God about them, we need to remember that these are our portal to glory. This is why the apostle Paul says, "I want to know Christ and the power of his resurrection and the fellowship of sharing in his sufferings" (Phil. 3:10) and why James tells us to "consider it pure joy" when we meet adversity (James 1:2). They recognize the intimate relationship between our suffering and our everlasting condition in heaven.

Scripture compares our emergence into the next world to childbirth. Jesus refers to the intense suffering that will precede his return as "birth pains" (Matt. 24:8), and Paul says, "the whole creation has been groaning as in the pains of childbirth" (Rom. 8:22). I was at my wife's side for the birth of each of our kids. Her labor was excruciating, and it seemed endless. But each time after the baby was born, I was struck by how quickly the pain and chaos turned to joy and celebration. The switch from agony to ecstasy was virtually instantaneous. This is a powerful — though I'm sure grossly inadequate — metaphor for what awaits us, and it helps me to better understand Paul's meaning when he says that "our present sufferings are not worth comparing with the glory that will be revealed in us" (Rom. 8:18).

Some of our suffering may seem so random or relentlessly brutal that we cannot imagine any good coming from it. Yet often we see these very trials redeemed in amazing ways. The story of Joni Eareckson Tada vividly illustrates how God can use an apparently senseless tragedy to bring about great good. When Joni was a young woman, she had a diving accident in the Chesapeake Bay that made her a quadriplegic. Initially, she despaired to the point of wanting to die, but God changed her through the influence of some caring friends. Soon she learned to paint by holding the brush with her teeth. Eventually she turned to writing, and today she is a widely acclaimed author and speaker whose words have helped millions of people.[44]

Tada says unreservedly that her diving accident was the best thing that ever happened to her. And many others would say the same about some of their most harrowing trials. This is the paradoxical nature of suffering for the Christian — God parleys pain into joy, evil into great blessing. But it should not surprise us that he does this for his children, because Jesus Christ is the paradigm. God brought the greatest good (the redemption of all humanity) out of the worst evil (the torture and murder of the Son of God). If God can do this, then what sin or suffering can he not redeem?

Yes, some situations are so devastating that it is hard to imagine what good could follow from them. But our inability to imagine what good God may bring out of our suffering is irrelevant to his actual ability to do so. We can know *that* something is so, even if we don't understand how. And even if we could conclude that a particular trial could never bring any further good in this world, it does not follow from this that God cannot do so in the next world and in an everlastingly wonderful way. We must trust his promise that "in all things God works for the good of those who love him" (Rom. 8:28). When he says all things, he means *all* things — from broken teeth to paralysis.

Many people do not take solace in the prospect of heaven because they doubt that it is even real. They consider it a mental crutch, a way of refusing to face up to the harsh reality of the human condition — that life is sad and frightening. Believing in heaven, they say, is just a way of dealing with our sorrow and fear. It is a fantasy that rational adults should grow out of.

But what if our fantasies were more realistic than we ever dreamed? What if our fears and sorrows were themselves signs that heaven is real? And what if children were more rational than many adults when it comes to our ultimate destiny?

17

The Way
Back Home

"Dad, I'm pregnant."

"Well, honey, do you want to keep the baby?"

"Of course I want the baby."

"If you change your mind, I'll give you five hundred dollars for the abortion."

This exchange actually took place between my mother and her dad when she was pregnant with me. At thirty-seven she was too old to have another baby, or so thought my grandfather. (I am the last of four kids.) For a time my mother shared this concern. When I was just a few months old, she took me in for a checkup and sat in the waiting room, looking around at the other mothers still in their twenties. Stepping into the exam room, she said to the pediatrician, "Sometimes I feel too old to have a baby." Pointing at the baby in her arms, the doctor replied, "*He* doesn't think you're too old." And that was the last time my mother gave it any thought.

Years later, when my grandfather came to the house for one of his late afternoon visits, he commented to my mother, in reference to his offer from years earlier, "Phyllis, every time I see little Jimmy, I feel so guilty."

"Dad, you *should* feel guilty," she said. "You know what I should have done?"

"What?"

"I should have taken the five hundred dollars and gone on a trip with that money. That's what I should have done."

"You really should have," he said. "It would have served me right."

When I try to consider the "what ifs" suggested by that story, my brain fails me. But it's really a waste of mental effort anyway, because there really is no sense in which my mother "might have" had the abortion. God had ordained all my days "before one of them came to be" (Ps. 139:16). Notwithstanding the schemes of my grandfather, or anyone else for that matter, God had his own plan, and this did not include my demise *in utero*. Rather, his intention was to weave my life among thousands of others, just as he was weaving me together in my mother's womb.

Now I contemplate the fact that my own kids' lives are divinely orchestrated as well, that they have destinies of their own, both chosen by and for them, likewise weaved into the fabric of a vast community of saints and sinners, heroes and villains. My children will know their own desperate sorrow, ecstatic joy, grinding boredom, and quiet satisfaction. They will laugh heartily, weep bitterly, sing, fight, dance, play, curse, joke, vote, make love, and consider the meaning of it all, like the rest of us do. And they will draw their own conclusions, like the rest of us do. Yes, their psyches will have been forged somewhat at the hands of their parents, again like the rest of us. Yet each of them is also irreducibly individual, a unique treasure of splendid personhood.

Parents are a pitiable lot; they lose no matter what. When parents fail to train their kids in the way they should go, their kids do not go the way they should and exasperate their parents. Of course, if the parents are not exasperated by their kids' waywardness, then they are worse than tragic. On the other hand, when parents do properly train their kids, their kids will think for themselves and undoubtedly make some missteps along the way — and exasperate their parents. But for those who parent well, there is abundant joy, through it all and afterward.

Jesus said, "Let the little children come to me, and do not hinder them, for the kingdom of God belongs to such as these" (Luke 18:16) and "No one can see the kingdom of God unless he is born again" (John 3:3). These expressions indicate that there is something about children that we should hope to retain even as we mature into adulthood. What is it? The answer is *not* moral innocence, as some would suggest. Children are sinners too, even if they are not particularly crafty in their immoral ways.

I think the answer has to do with other traits that are natural to children but which tend to wear off as we grow. For one thing, children have tremendous curiosity because the world is new to them and this gives rise to a fascination with even the simplest things. As adults we often dismiss this fascination as immature just because it is so pronounced in children. The fact is that the world is just as fascinating as kids find it to be.

Another crucial childlike trait is humility. Kids are low on the social ladder, and they know it. They are quite aware that they don't know much and that they aren't the ones who should be leading the family or neighborhood.[45] They look up to adults to lead them and are, for the most part, willing to follow ... that is, until they are ordered to take a nap or eat eggplant. For this reason, kids are more likely than adults to admit when they are wrong. The humility of children is connected to their inclination to have faith. They trust adults because they have to, because they are completely dependent on us and otherwise helpless in this world.

If only we adults could retain these childlike qualities of curiosity, humility, and faith. Instead, as we age our tendency is to lose these traits and even to develop vices opposite them: jadedness, pride, and cynicism.

If only we could be more childlike in our curiosity and rediscover our capacity to be fascinated by the world around us, however familiar it might seem to us. If only we could see how low we really are relative to the greatness of God, to be more willing to follow his orders and admit when we are wrong. If only we could comprehend how utterly dependent we are upon our heavenly Father and how helpless we are to make it on our own in this world.

While doing the dishes one day, I glanced out the kitchen window and noticed Bailey, Sam, and three of the Shutt kids — Ivy, Josephine, and Elijah — huddled together on the side of the road. They were looking down at something and poking it with a stick. I figured that, whatever it was, they'd soon tire of it and then go on to something else. But that didn't happen. The longer they stood there, the more interested they became in whatever it was they were examining. So I decided to go out and see what it was that captivated them so.

When I stepped outside, Bailey called me over, saying "Dad, come quick! You need to help us!"

"What is it?" I asked, walking over to them.

"Look, this squirrel just died," said Elijah.

"Yeah, he was just hit by a car. Ivy and I saw it. Dad, it's so sad. Can we bury him somewhere?" asked Bailey.

"We were going to bury him in our yard, but we buried another squirrel there the other day," explained Ivy, pointing toward her house. "I don't think we can do another one yet. My dad wouldn't like that."

"We can bury him in our yard," I said.

"Really?" said Sam, his hands fidgeting with excitement.

"Where?" asked Bailey.

"Um, how about where those tall, skinny flowers bloom near the garage each spring?" I carefully avoided mentioning the name of the flower species — naked ladies. This was not a moment for jokes or silly distractions.

"Okay, let's take him over," Bailey said, reaching down to pick up the squirrel.

"No, buddy, let me do that," I cautioned. I bent over, grabbing the tip of the tail. He was large, with a very bushy tail. It was autumn, and he had fattened himself up for winter. "Follow me, guys," I said, walking toward our yard. "Bailey, get me a shovel from the garage."

As we prepared to dig the squirrel's grave, the Shutt girls were called home, leaving Bailey, Sam, Elijah, and me to do the job. The boys asked if they could help with the digging, and I let them each take turns. When it was deep enough, I placed the squirrel in the hole and asked them if they'd like to have a funeral service. They all said yes, so several of us prayed for the squirrel.

Sam bowed his head and said, "Dear God, please don't let him be hurt anymore." He paused, said, "Amen," then looked at his brother expectantly.

Bailey followed, "Lord, thank you so much for this beautiful creature, and we pray that he will be okay in heaven. Please let him have lots of friends there. Amen."

I know some Christian parents who avoid talking to their kids about death. They believe a young child will be disturbed by the subject, so it's best to wait until they are more mature. My wife and I take a different view of the matter. If a kid is mature enough to ask a substantive question, we figure they are mature enough to handle a truthful response.

This policy was put to the test shortly after Maggie was born. When we changed her diaper, Bailey noticed that she doesn't have a penis, and he asked us why. After that he began to ask even more probing questions about body parts, so we decided to tell him the facts of life. We frankly gave him all of the basic information, without any sense of embarrassment. He listened intently, and when we were finished we asked if he had any questions. Bailey pondered for a few moments, then looked up and said, "Why don't trees talk?" We smiled and answered that question too. Then he went out to play.

He didn't ask us any more questions about babies or genitalia for many months, and we began to worry that perhaps he had some negative feelings about the subject. But further conversations revealed that his curiosity had been satisfied and he simply had no more questions. As Bailey has grown older, we have felt confirmed in our approach. We don't want him to learn the facts of life from a friend or classmate in a haphazard, insensitive way. On top of this, it is good for his worldview development to know how God brings people into this world. The facts of reproduction are crucial to understanding human nature, the divine nature, and how we are related. We figure that the earlier a child can get going in understanding these things, the better.

Few subjects are more important or interesting than questions about our origin and destiny as human beings. Where did we come from? And where are we going? Answer these two questions and you have essentially discovered life's meaning. No wonder, then, we find these questions so interesting. And no wonder they are so contentious when discussed in public. The implications of one's answers could not be greater, pertaining to every area of human conduct and the possibility of finding happiness in life. At the end of the day, there are only two basic orientations one may take regarding these questions: human life has transcendent meaning, or it does not. Either life's purpose is determined from without, by our ultimate Source, or from within, by us.

But if we can find no further purpose to our existence than what we give to it, then life really has no ultimate meaning. Life, as Shakespeare put it, is "a tale told by an idiot, full of sound and fury, signifying nothing."[46] Scramble as we might to conjure some significance for ourselves as we hurtle toward the grave, it is all a waste. Back we go to the nothingness from which we came. So even our best efforts to affirm the value of anything along the way are a pathetic self-deception.

Shakespeare's choice of the theatrical metaphor for human life is a good one. For those of us who believe in God, it is natural to think of God as a sort of playwright, a narrator in whose cosmic drama we find ourselves. This model naturally invites us to think about all of life in terms of purpose. Good storytellers, after all, develop themes, and they make every detail serve the theme in some way. They also fill the story with surprising twists and turns, making for a kind of puzzle. In fact, the more puzzling, the more beautiful, so long as in the end the purpose is made plain. It is interesting to see how Scripture affirms this point about our world, as Paul declares, "Now we see but a poor reflection as in a mirror; then we shall see face to face. Now I know in part; then I shall know fully, even as I am fully known" (1 Cor. 13:12).

A while back, Bailey expressed a desire to hug God. I think this captures the deepest yearning within all of us — to return to our Source, to embrace the one from whom our very being flows, and to know him who fully knows us. If the belonging that we feel in relation to our parents is primal, then how much more so must be our sense of belonging to God? We are his offspring in an incomparably deeper way than we are children of our earthly parents. But since that yearning is *so* deep and otherworldly, we don't recognize it for what it is.

The existentialist philosophers have come closest to actually describing it, though they could do so only in negative terms. Kierkegaard referred to it with the concept of dread, and Sartre touched upon it with the notion of alienation, a certain sense that one is not where one should be. It takes the form of a vague unease that we feel all of the time, no matter how well things are going for us. However content or happy we might be, there is always that abiding feeling that something is not right, that we aren't fully connected or in touch with what is most real or meaningful.

To be a Christian is, among other things, to recognize this dread or alienation as symptoms of our rebellion. Faith conversion is essentially a process of coming to realize that Christ is the path back to our Source, from whom we have become tragically disconnected. He is the Way Back Home. All of us share in this quest to find our way home. Not all of us recognize that this is what preoccupies us, but it is our common lot as fallen human beings. Some find the way, while others do not.

Many of us are given foretastes of our home through various experiences, such as by contemplating some spiritual truth or reuniting with a loved one. When these experiences are especially exquisite, we weep. C. S. Lewis noted that this reveals how joy is actually a species of sorrow. We cry when we are very joyful because we are weak and are overwhelmed by the realization — though it is typically subconscious — that we are not yet home. Even without having been there, we already miss our eternal abode and the heavenly fellowship awaiting us there. Perhaps one of the reasons we'll need resurrection bodies is so that we'll be able to withstand the relentless joy of the next world. It's simply too much beauty and happiness for a fallen soul to take.

Epilogue

Recently it became clear to us that Mac had out-grown his ten-gallon terrarium, so we moved him into a much larger one. We also added a few accou-trements, including a gecko hammock, calcium sand, and something called a humid hive, where he can go to moisturize his skin when he molts. Amy and the kids have also talked me into expanding our gecko experi-ment. Our plan is to purchase a female gecko. After raising her in a separate enclosure until she reaches maturity, we will introduce her to Mac and let (virtual) nature take its course. While it is possible that they will hate each other and fight to the death, our hope is that they will hit it off and reproduce. So chances are that as you read this, there is a booming gecko community at our house. I certainly hope so. I think Mac would enjoy being a dad.

I value your thoughts about what you've just read.
Please share them with me. You'll find contact information
in the back of this book.

Acknowledgments

If the writing of any book is an adventure, this one has been a jungle safari — complete with bumps, bruises, and bafflement, adorned with plenty of wildlife, human and otherwise, and sprinkled with a dash of domestic fauna for good measure.

I want to thank all of my neighbors, friends, and bygone acquaintances who made appearances in this book. All of us are supporting actors in some narrative or other.

Thanks to my brother Robert, who has taught me more about writing than anyone. And I remain grateful to my longtime friend Dan Newcomb, whose loyalty I will always cherish. Somehow he knew I was a writer before I did.

Thanks to all the good people at New Life Presbyterian Church in Yorktown, Indiana, especially my pastor and friend, Bob O'Bannon. And here's a shout-out to my colleagues and students at Taylor University for their remarkable energy and support. Ours is a truly inspiring community of pilgrims, pursuing the life of the mind ... and beyond.

Thanks to my wife, Amy, whose contributions to this project were myriad. Though she functioned variously as co-author, editor, and proofreader, she has humbly refused all of those titles. That's probably a good thing, since it keeps things simpler for the publisher.

Speaking of whom, the folks at Zondervan have been wonderful. Rumors of their professional expertise have not been exaggerated. I am immensely indebted to Angela Scheff for her creative vision for this project and her fastidious editorial work. Thanks also to Brian Phipps. It has been a pleasure and an honor to benefit from his eagle eye.

I owe a huge debt of gratitude to Robert, Andrew, and Erik at Wolgemuth and Associates, Inc., especially Andrew, whose literary midwifery is a thing of beauty.

Finally, I want to thank my children for being unwitting contributors to this project. Every word, wink, and nod has been perfectly on cue. And every question has made my mind work a little harder, while making my life a little richer. They continue to teach the teacher.

By the way, did any of you feed the gecko?

Notes

1. According to Greek mythology, the gods punished Sisyphus, the deceitful king of Ephyra, by making him carry a giant stone up a steep hill. However, just before reaching the hilltop each time, the boulder would elude him and fall back into the valley, after which he would retrieve the stone only to start the frustrating cycle over again.
2. Martin Heidegger, *Introduction to Metaphysics* (New Haven, Conn.: Yale Univ. Press, 2000), chap. 1.
3. These doctrines are actually specific to Upanishadic Hinduism. Many folks in the Hindu tradition believe in a personal God and reject an absolute pantheism.
4. I should add that since God is also immanent, he is "in" time as well. So he can "anticipate" or "look forward to" events as we do. But he is not limited to this temporal perspective.
5. Ps. 19:1.
6. Rom. 1:20.
7. Rom. 1:18.
8. This phrase refers to the title of Richard Dawkins' book *The God Delusion* (New York: Houghton Mifflin, 2006).
9. I want to clarify that my point here is not primarily about the Calvinist-Arminian debate, though it might have implications for that issue. I am just observing that we don't choose our beliefs, regardless of the subject. Consider your beliefs about everything from your favorite football team to the morality of the death penalty. You cannot change *any* of these beliefs through a simple act of will. Even if I bribed you to take a different view about one of them, you couldn't do it. That's because beliefs are not something that you choose.
10. A common Protestant view, known as the penal-substitutionary theory, declares that Christ's righteousness is simply imputed to us, applied to us purely by an act of divine fiat. But there are two major problems with this view.

One is the fact that it is unjust — treating one person's works as if they belonged to another person. The other problem is that this theory can't make sense of the transformation of humanity which the work of Christ is supposed to achieve. That is, even if it could account for our past sins, this theory can't make sense of how Christ's work enables us to overcome future sins.

11. See Col. 1:18, 24; Rom. 12:5; Eph. 4:4; John 15:5 – 8.
12. You can check out some of their chirping sounds at the Global Gecko Association website: http://www.gekkota.com/. This site features helpful information for anyone with an interest in geckos, from hobbyists to herpetologists.
13. Molting in geckos and other lizards differs from that in snakes. Lizards shed their skin gradually in pieces. Snakes, being legless, can simply crawl out of their old skin, leaving it fully intact, though inside out, like pulling a sock off a foot. This might be the sole benefit of their curse.
14. Isaiah even refers to the "bread of adversity and the water of affliction" (Isa. 30:20), which suggests that from a spiritual standpoint, our trials *nourish* us.
15. As for a spiritual application for lizards eating their dead skin, I'm afraid I have none. I'll leave that to you — or your kids — to figure out.
16. Confucius, *The Analects*, trans. D. C. Lau (London: Penguin, 1979), 135.
17. Cultural factors may sometimes play into this as well. For example, the phrase "born again" is humorous, though its creative genius is all but lost on us today because of overuse.
18. Toward the end of his life, my own father's faith began to bloom and he came to a much firmer belief in God than he had known earlier in his life. But he struggled to believe in miracles, most significantly the virgin birth of Jesus. At one point, exasperated with himself, he asked my mother, "Why is it so easy for you and Jim to believe, but it is so hard for me?" I found this question encouraging, as it reminded me of the man who once exclaimed to Jesus, "I do believe; help me overcome my unbelief!" (Mark 9:24).

19. A student of mine once informed me that her father's umbilical scar healed so perfectly that he had no belly button. This caused him a great deal of embarrassment as he grew up, so he actually had a "normal" navel surgically created.
20. The distinction between essential and common qualities is an old one. But in applying it to rebut this objection to the doctrine of Christ, I am indebted to Thomas Morris. See his excellent book *The Logic of God Incarnate* (Ithaca, N.Y.: Cornell Univ. Press, 1986), chap. 3.
21. See also Col. 1:16 and Phil. 2:6.
22. 1 John 1:5.
23. John 8:12.
24. Matt. 17:1–6.
25. See, for example, Ezek. 1:27 and Rev. 1:16.
26. Even the angel's question is a bit comical. Why are they looking into the sky? Because a human being—the Son of God, no less—just floated up there, *that's why*!
27. He does so, in fact, no less than seven times in Genesis 1.
28. This is not to deny that human beings are free and morally responsible. Scripture teaches both that God is sovereign and that human beings are responsible for their actions. While some theologies emphasize one of these truths at the expense of the other, a biblically balanced view affirms both. For an extensive discussion of this issue, see my book *The Benefits of Providence: A New Look at Divine Sovereignty* (Wheaton, Ill.: Crossway, 2005).
29. The song is titled "From a Distance" (1993). Musically, it is sentimental schmaltz, but hey, at least the theology is bad.
30. For example, see Exod. 7:3; Deut. 6:22; Neh. 9:10; Ps. 135:9; Jer. 32:20–21; Dan. 6:27; John 4:48; and Acts 14:3.
31. After all, God is a necessary being, the sort of being for whom it would be impossible to go out of existence or, for that matter, to have had a beginning.
32. See Deut. 18:10–12 and Gal. 5:20.
33. 1 Samuel 28.
34. In ancient Israel such practice warranted the death penalty. See Lev. 20:27.

35. See Matt. 24:36 and Luke 8:43–48.
36. For example, think of your mother's maiden name. You weren't thinking of it, but now you are. I triggered your mental access to that fact. You had the knowledge all along, but it became part of your conscious awareness (again) when I prompted you.
37. Isa. 11:6–7.
38. See 1 Cor. 15:35–44 and 2 Cor. 5:1–4.
39. Eccl. 3:11.
40. Thomas Aquinas argued for the immortality of the soul on the basis of the universal desire for immortality. All natural desires are capable of being fulfilled, he claimed, and since immortality is a natural human desire, it must be capable of being satisfied.
41. As for popular images of hell, many of them feature parties, swarms of people being naughty together, essentially continuing their earthly lifestyle of indulgence, albeit in the midst of a higher (though not necessarily painful) ambient temperature. And monitoring the proceedings, usually off to one side, is the devil himself — a red-suited jesterlike creature, complete with pitchfork and tail — harmless and amusing. This inversion of truth is every bit as complete as the popular image of heaven.
42. See Ps. 145:20; Gal. 6:8; and 2 Thess. 1:9.
43. Note the terminology here, by the way — specifically the writer's use of the word *obey* as opposed to *faith*. The two are really interchangeable. Faith and obedience imply one another.
44. If you want to check out Tada's inspiring story, read her book *Joni* (Grand Rapids: Zondervan, 2001).
45. Some non-adults do think they know everything and that, in fact, they should rule the world. They are called teenagers.
46. *Macbeth*, act 5, scene 5.

Share Your Thoughts

With the Author: Your comments will be forwarded to
the author when you send them to *zauthor@zondervan.com*.

With Zondervan: Submit your review of this book
by writing to *zreview@zondervan.com*.

Free Online Resources at
www.zondervan.com/hello

 Zondervan AuthorTracker: Be notified whenever your
favorite authors publish new books, go on tour, or post
an update about what's happening in their lives.

 Daily Bible Verses and Devotions: Enrich your life
with daily Bible verses or devotions that help you start
every morning focused on God.

 Free Email Publications: Sign up for newsletters on
fiction, Christian living, church ministry, parenting, and
more.

 Zondervan Bible Search: Find and compare
Bible passages in a variety of translations at
www.zondervanbiblesearch.com.

 Other Benefits: Register yourself to receive online
benefits like coupons and special offers, or to participate
in research.